Smoke
Gets in Your Eyes

Branding and Design

in Cigarette Packaging

MICHAEL THIBODEAU & JANA MARTIN

Abbeville Press Publishers

New York   London   Paris

Contents

Preface

Michael Thibodeau

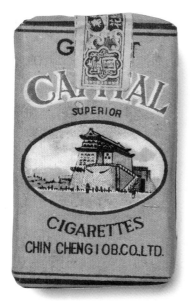

Great Capital (*ABOVE*)
Chin Cheng Tobacco Co., China,
1930s

Da Quen Meng (*Grand Gate*)
(*BELOW*)
China, 1995

IT WAS WHILE TRAVELING that I first became interested in the incredible diversity of cigarette branding. In each country I visited, the cigarette brands seemed to reflect cultural aspirations more than any characteristics of the tobacco product itself. In Cambodia, a poor and war-torn nation, I found Luxury and Victory cigarette brands. The French rarely confess a desire for American products, yet they buy Brooklyn cigarettes. Chinese culture discourages public displays of the self—except on a package of cigarettes. How surprising that in the country that adopted the monotonous Mao suit thousands of cigarette brands are marketed to so many different individual tastes and desires.

Why are there literally thousands of international brands for paper-rolled tobacco, and why aren't these brands more descriptive of the product itself? After all, tobacco is a crop, grown just like lettuce or broccoli. But watch people in supermarkets. They squeeze the tomatoes, scrutinize the apples, frown over limp spinach. But once at the checkout counter, they know exactly which brand of cigarettes they want, without a second look. In our day, that choice has little to do with the actual cigarette, or with the painstaking, labor-consuming process of growing the tobacco. Selection has to do with linking the cigarette to the aspirations of the smoker.

Like many things taboo to teenagers—alcohol, coffee, automobiles, sex—cigarettes are part of the rite of passage to adult life. The practice of smoking is imbued with the same novelty and drama as everything else happening during that time of transition. The messages conveyed by certain brands are absorbed during these impressionable years, and for adults looking back, those brands come to represent a part of their adult identity. It is no wonder that cigarette brands enjoy some of the highest brand loyalty in consumer marketing. Once a smoker embraces a brand, he or she is not likely to switch.

This loyalty helps explain why packs seldom change over the years. The Chesterfield pack of today is very much the same as it was nearly a hundred years ago. This tendency to keep the symbolic elements of a brand unchanged holds true around the world. By chance I came across two different packages of Chinese Great Capital cigarettes, separated by sixty years. Even though the cigarettes inside have become mass products, refined, extended, and filtered over time, the core image of the brand's design remains the same.

As the twentieth century progressed, manufacturers learned a key lesson in branding and package design: any changes should be weighed very carefully.

The manufacturer of Lucky Strike, for instance, conducted an array of market surveys in 1940–41 on what would happen if the pack changed from green to white. Only after ample research showed that the color shift would be to the brand's advantage did the company go ahead. The industrial designer Raymond Loewy is credited with the pack's dramatic metamorphosis, but there was really nothing dramatic about it. The typography stayed the same. The color change had already been determined before Loewy signed his contract. The production department knew exactly how much would be saved by eschewing the costly green ink for white, and the CEO had seen a thorough mock-up of the new package, made by company designers, before Loewy came on. What did Loewy do? Changed the banding around the target, made sure the white was white. In the increasingly sophisticated arena of cigarette packaging by the American Big Tobacco companies, that was plenty.

Lucky Strike (ABOVE, LEFT)
American Tobacco Co., U.S.A., 1925; originally introduced in 1917

Lucky Strike (ABOVE, RIGHT)
American Tobacco Co., U.S.A., 1995; package redesigned by Raymond Loewy in 1942

Cigarette brands may not describe their contents, but they do describe the stuff that is paramount to our lives. With as many facets as human character, they range from Life to Death, from Go to Stop, Impartial to Particular. There's Friend, Peace, Hope, and Double Happiness. Sometimes they embody the qualities we wish we had, the lives we wish we could lead, the great escapes we wish we could make. Look at the Turkish cigarette packs from the early twentieth century: their exotic harem girls and fierce-looking sultans are rich with sensual fantasy.

I find it delightful that so many cigarette packages reflect a design sensibility that has little to do with cautious planning, as if the design sprang from a moment of pure inspiration. Some of these designs have transcended the changing times, such as the eternally popular Camel, which started with a photograph of an aggravated pack animal (although how the company later maintained the brand's popularity had nothing to do with sudden inspiration). Some brands lasted only as long as the fashions and mind-sets of their era, such as the joyous Pink, a Japanese postwar pack with a bright pink coat, or a gorgeous Soviet pack, called simply U.S.S.R., which shows a worker holding up a crimson star in a moody, dark blue setting. Whether a one-off or a classic brand, and whatever part of the world it comes from, each package has been designed to embody an aspiration of the culture that created it.

Life (BELOW, LEFT)
Brown & Williamson Tobacco Corp., U.S.A., c. 1950

Black Death (BELOW, RIGHT)
Black Death U.S.A., 1991

ZIRA
CIGARETTES

THIS BOX
FRONT HAS
NO
REDEMPTION
VALUE

NEBO

CIGARETTES

CORK TIP

THIS BOX
FRONT HAS
NO
REDEMPTION
VALUE

Introduction
A Brief History of Cigarette Packaging

AN EIGHTEEN-YEAR-OLD INVENTOR FROM VIRGINIA STARTED IT ALL, which is entirely appropriate for an industry whose origins were so closely tied to that state and whose most reliable market has always been young men. It was 1878, during an era when new machines were being invented every day—sewing machines, steam-driven combines, a box telephone that could transmit voices. Young James Bonsack heard that the Richmond, Virginia, tobacco company Allen & Ginter was willing to pay $75,000 to the first man who could invent a fast cigarette-rolling machine. While his friends were out stealing kisses or daydreaming through college algebra, Bonsack got to work.

The history of cigarette packaging before Bonsack's machine has its own milestones, but nothing compares to the remarkable synergy of mass production, packaging, marketing, and transportation that his machine would spark. Before mechanization, tobacco smoking had caught fire very slowly. The first recorded evidence traces back to 6000 B.C., when the plant flourished in the pre-Columbian Americas; by 1 B.C., indigenous peoples smoked tobacco, chewed tobacco, and brewed it for hallucinogenic enemas. Some six hundred to a thousand years later the Mayans were smoking tobacco leaves rolled up and tied with string, as shown in a pottery vessel from Guatemala. The Mayan word for smoking, *si kar,* provided the basis for the modern word *cigar,* just as the indigenous San Salvadoran word for their tobacco pipes, *tobago,* became our word *tobacco.* The growing popularity of cigars and pipes in sixteenth- and seventeenth-century Europe created the need for tobacco plantations. Europeans having decided, for various reasons, that growing tobacco was an unsavory undertaking, they relegated these plantations to the colonies. Tobacco, which can grow in many climates, would take well to the colonies' rich, fertile soil.

Virginia in the 1600s had an unruly reputation until John Rolfe (also known as Pocahontas's husband) began to cultivate the leaf there. Tobacco soon permeated every facet of the state's affairs and gave it economic respectability. When shiploads of maidens arrived from England to marry the up-and-coming new tobacco farmers, the fee for their passage was paid in tobacco, the reigning currency. Commercial tobacco interests also influenced politics: Virginians saw the real issue of the Revolutionary War as tobacco and readily admitted that their fortunes depended on slaves to grow their labor-intensive crops.

Zira AND *Nebo* (OPPOSITE)
P. Lorillard Tobacco Co., U.S.A.;
introduced in 1911

Sweet Gold Clip (*ABOVE*)
S. F. Hess & Co., U.S.A., c. 1880

Dixie (*BELOW*)
Allen & Ginter Tobacco Co.,
U.S.A., 1891

When, in 1839, a North Carolina slave forgot to close the curing shed flue, a new way to cure leaves was discovered. Tobacco farmers began curing their tobacco using this method, which produced a lighter-leafed tobacco. This new variety came to be known as Virginia Bright. The fact that it was far milder than any other varieties encouraged smokers to inhale, thus changing the experience of smoking. Once in the lungs, nicotine from the smoke flooded the bloodstream, yielding that mysterious sense of well-being now known as a nicotine high.

European taste still tended toward the darker Turkish tobacco, which had been transplanted in the 1600s from the Americas to Mediterranean fields. France's tobacco monopoly began manufacturing Turkish cigarettes in 1843; English tobacconist Philip Morris included them among his wares beginning in 1847. Germany lifted its last restrictions against tobacco in 1848. The Crimean War (1854-56) introduced British soldiers to the cheap paper-tube cigarettes—*papirassi*—smoked by their Turkish allies. They took them back to England, where the aura of bravery surrounding the soldiers helped make their new cigarettes a British fad. The brands of the 1850s and 1860s included Sweet Threes, made in England's first cigarette factory (run by war veteran Robert Gloag). Like most packs of the day, they were wrapped in printed tissue paper that was either glued or twisted closed.

The fledgling cigarette industry was still provincial in scale, but growing. Aiming to steal some of the fire from the well-established cigar market, cigarette makers were helped along in the U.S. by such factors as rising taxes, which drove cigar prices out of reach for many, and safety matches, invented in 1852, which made lighting up quick and convenient. Early packaging wasn't yet distinct—wrappers bore the same muted colors as other consumables—but the drive to market cigarettes was already developing. Advertising display cards showed smokers in scenes of leisure and comfort. In 1860 the American cigarette maker P. Lorillard created a stir by secreting $100 bills into select packages of his blended Century rolling tobacco, as a gimmick to celebrate the company's one hundredth birthday. The fostering of brand recognition was furthered in the 1870s, when roadside stands, local shops, and city streets were plastered with advertisements for Bull Durham rolling tobacco.

Allen & Ginter employed a workforce of nimble-fingered young women to roll their cigarettes, and the faster girls could roll four a minute. Competitor James Buchanan Duke, an ambitious North Carolinian from a tobacco-farming family, brought trainloads of European immigrants down from New York City to staff his factory; wary of labor problems, he paid eager attention to any talk of mechanization. But it was Allen & Ginter whose prize money bought James Bonsack's lightning-fast cigarette-rolling machine and made the young inventor a rich man.

Adapting to mechanization turned out not to be easy. Bonsack's hands-free machine, with its intricate system of guillotines and chutes, spit out 120,000 cigarettes a day, ten times more than any firm, anywhere, had ever been able to produce. Suddenly Allen & Ginter was facing an unexpected crisis: there were just too many cigarettes to sell. Fearful of going under, the firm returned, temporarily, to the safer routine of hand rolling. And that gave "Buck" Duke an opportunity as wide as the sea. It's said that when he first heard about Bonsack's machine, Duke asked for an atlas, pointed to the place with the largest population concentration in the world—China—and announced, "Gentlemen, this is where we will sell cigarettes." In 1884 he made a deal with Bonsack. In exchange for helping Bonsack refine the still-testy machine with the help of W. Duke Sons & Company mechanics, Duke could purchase the machine at 25 percent less than the price paid by any competitor. The magnate readily agreed to buy as many machines as he could, and cigarette production took its quantum leap.

Cigarette industry executives tend to go misty-eyed when reminiscing about Duke; he never worried about whether a market was there—he'd just make one. And from the beginning his ambitions were global. He shifted his headquarters north to Manhattan and set up a national system of manufacturing, distributing, and marketing. He hired young men to work as sales representatives throughout the country, in both cities and rural areas, saturating the market and building up a national appetite for cigarettes to match the vastly increased supply created by mass production. In a few years Duke would launch export and production operations in China and other foreign territories as well, creating one of the earliest multinational corporations.

In 1886, with his Bonsack machines producing 744 million cigarettes a year, Duke launched a number of brands in the American market, each positioned with its own identity and appeal. In so doing, he helped the American market discover that it had individual tastes. Duke's Cross Cut was a working-man's smoke, featuring a two-man saw cutting diagonally across the pack. Preferred Stock, a more upscale variety, features a Wall Street ticker unfurling tape that promises "20 Shares." Duke of Durham was a playful jab at the old standard, Bull Durham; Duke presented his brand as the hand-rolling tobacco's savvier younger cousin. Cameo, an ornately packaged brand, reflects the genteel Victorian fashions of the day.

The Cameo package is notable for its trompe l'oeil device, which cleverly takes advantage of the hull-and-shell structure of the packet, in which the cigarettes sit in a cardboard hull that's enclosed in a wraparound shell. On the Cameo pack, the shell is printed with the image of a fashionable cameo ring; one slips off the ring to reach the cigarettes in the hull. The visionary Duke saw package design as an opportunity to capture the buyer's imagination as well as his nickel. He had perfected the more durable packet structure to with-

Duke's Cameo
American Tobacco Co., U.S.A.,
c. 1890; introduced in 1884

stand the rigors of mass distribution, though for some brands he still employed the weaker but established package of paper wrapping with cardboard stiffeners. To improve on that, he popularized the practice of printing inventions or portraits of athletes and actresses on the stiffener cards. Competitors would soon do the same, aided by new advances in lithography and inexpensive photoreproduction techniques. They inserted not only collectible cards but also tiny framed portraits, photographs, or even squares of silk that could be redeemed for larger swaths. The idea of repeat buying of a specific brand was thus lodged in smokers' minds, spurred by the desire to collect and reinforced by the addictive nature (as yet undiscovered but suspected by a few) of smoking.

Duke's arrangement with Bonsack didn't prohibit his competitors from using the machine; they just had to pay more than he did. In 1887, certain of his advantage, he slashed prices, underselling everyone. Within two years the other top U.S. firms—among them, Lorillard, Liggett & Myers, and R. J. Reynolds—were forced to join with Duke or be put out of business. The result was American Tobacco Company (ATC), whose president—or Duke—was none other than Duke.

The cigarette industry in England favored a different sensibility. Philip Morris's shop and its new neighbor, Benson & Hedges, focused on handmade cigarettes, a safe bet for their traditionalist London clientele. The British belief that handmade meant higher quality influenced the packaging schemes of the new mass-produced cigarettes. In 1888 the firm of W. D. & H. O. Wills bought a Bonsack and launched Britain's first machine-made brands, Wild Woodbine and Cinderella, both of which linked heritage with modernity in their designs. Wild Woodbine, named after a medicinal herb, features Arts and Crafts motifs. Cinderella used the fairy tale to convey the message that a humble appearance cloaked equal, if not superior, quality.

By 1890 both the American Tobacco Company and various British tobacco companies began selling cigarettes to the rest of the world. England exported its cigarettes to Africa, Southeast Asia, and India. ATC, under Duke's supervision, began exporting to China and Japan, staffing sales and distribution offices with the same type of enterprising young men he'd employed in his American branches. In turn-of-the-century Japan an ATC salesman converted large populations of native *kiseru* pipe smokers to ATC's American brands. The salesman didn't speak a word of Japanese, but the packages and products spoke for themselves—symbols of the West at a time when Japan had once again turned its attention to the outside world.

Cigarettes went to Central and South America through Europe, becoming fashionable in cities where European expatriates followed the trends back home. In Chile in the 1890s a local manufacturer created Cigarrillos Tony, fea-

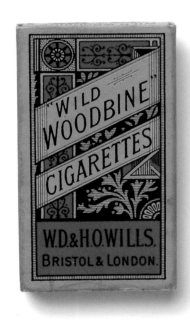

Wild Woodbine
W. D. & H. O. Wills, U.K.,
c. 1930; introduced
in 1888

turing an androgynous dandy in formal dress, with
clownishly elongated feet and a tiny top hat perched on
his head. Smoke from his cigarette wafts into the air,
forming the letters *que rico* (how rich). The whole image
is framed in Art Nouveau swirls. In Europe, Tony Clubs
were where independent-minded women went to smoke
in peace. Were Tony cigarettes a sideways reference to
those women, awkwardly defiant in their men's suits?
The very condensed nature of cigarette package design
called for such stacking references: a whole range of
associations compressed onto the surface of a three-
inch-tall box.

Tony
Chile, c. 1900

By the turn of the century, Duke's company con-
trolled 90 percent of the American market. ATC con-
tinued to manufacture, package, and sell the same brands originated by the
companies it had absorbed, exporting millions of cartons to markets overseas,
particularly in Asia. British manufacturers, leery of Duke's success and fearful
that ATC would expand into the U.K. market, consolidated into Imperial
Tobacco in 1901. Within a year the two conglomerates had formed British-
American Tobacco (BAT), forging a trade agreement that allowed each to con-
trol its own markets while trying to assert sovereignty as a united partnership
over Asian markets as well.

BAT flooded the overseas markets, particularly Japan and China, not only
with cigarettes but also with offices, factories, and salesmen. Instead of trying to compete with BAT, the Japanese tobacco firm Murai entered into a partnership with it; their brands, featuring Western imagery, were popular among
urban Japanese. Another company, Iwaya, played up Japanese traditions with
such brands as Tengu, which was named for the red-faced goblin of Japanese
mythology. In 1904 the Meiji government took over the tobacco industry to
protect it from BAT's infiltration, using tariffs and distribution restrictions to
effectively close the archipelago to imports. One of the established brands it
continued to circulate (originally produced by the Isegu company) was an
overt copy of BAT's enduring brand John Player. The Japanese version featured
a nearly identical design, complete with rugged naval hero and Gothic type-
face. But, perhaps reflecting confusion over the difference between *r* and *l* in
the English language, the brand is called John Prayer.

The Japanese Tobacco Monopoly would continue to exclude foreign
brands until 1945, and it did not fully open up its market until the 1980s. BAT
had better luck in China, where it sparked fierce competition with the Chinese
Nanyang Brothers, but it did have to endure periods of intense anti-foreign
sentiment there that resulted in boycotts and demonstrations. As BAT's skill in

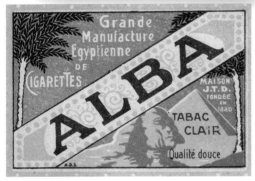

Camel *(ABOVE, TOP)*
R. J. Reynolds, U.S.A., 1920s;
introduced in 1913

Alba *(ABOVE, BOTTOM)*
Maison J. T. D., Belgium, c. 1900

Pyrgos *(BELOW)*
A. Johnson & Co., U.S.A., c. 1915

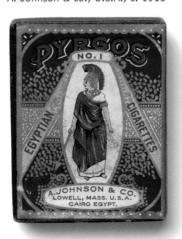

adapting to Chinese culture increased, so did its use of symbols and simple, obvious designs in its export packages. Animal figures were adapted, from tigers to birds, and sales representatives were instructed to test the reaction to designs in different provinces. Between 1902 and 1912 sales of BAT cigarettes in China soared from 1.25 billion to 9.75 billion.

In the U.S., Duke's long run was coming to an end, and after his vast ATC monopoly was dissolved in 1911 by the Sherman Antitrust Commission, he went to London to run BAT. ATC was divided into many smaller firms, including American Tobacco, Liggett & Myers, and P. Lorillard. Each invested its efforts in a few major brands, having learned that too many little brands confused the market and kept the flame of consumer recognition from igniting sales. Recognizability, not esoteric novelty, was what would sell cigarettes in this quickly evolving industry.

After ATC's breakup, another tobacco leader, R. J. Reynolds, swore that he would one-up Duke's success, saying, "Now watch me give him hell." Capitalizing on the attraction of Turkish cigarettes and the rage for things Egyptian, his advertisements announcing the new Camel cigarettes saturated the market for months before stores saw any product. The pack features a simple desert scene, with its namesake standing in front of two pyramids and an oasis. Restrained typography spells out the brand. There's not that much going on, yet the design somehow conveys a distinctive personality. In part, this is due to accident: the irritable camel being used as a model expressed its disdain just as the shutter clicked to take its portrait. In part, it's also due to the eye-catchingly clean composition. The brand would become the first American standard, winning Camels a seemingly eternal share of the market.

Other companies also played to the Orientalism then in vogue and to the preference among the moneyed and cultured set for Turkish cigarettes, with more ornately designed, less successful brands. In Belgium, Maison J. Tirou-Dirico's Alba brand of the early 1900s features a wizened sphinx and naively stylized trees—a little bit Greek, a little bit Egyptian, but still entirely exotic. Pyrgos—introduced in 1910 by a Massachusetts manufacturer with additional headquarters in Cairo, Egypt (as the box solemnly states)—uses another hybrid: a helmeted Greek warrior juxtaposed with the declaration "Egyptian Cigarettes." Lorillard brought out his and hers Turkish blends in 1911: Zira for women and Nebo for men (page 8).

The women's market was an important one, and Lorillard, like many other companies, tried packaging that had a slightly mysterious appeal. That approach reflects the early bafflement about how to reach women, who weren't even supposed to smoke in public. In 1904 a Manhattan woman smoking in her car was stopped by a consternated policeman who loudly exclaimed, "You can't smoke on Fifth Avenue, lady!" But women did smoke, and everyone knew it. For decades firms tried to offer

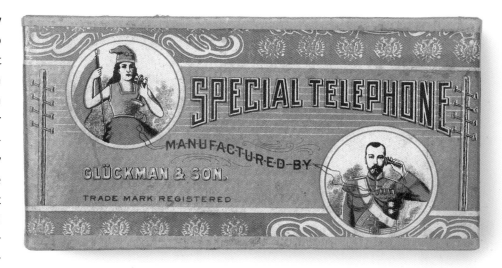

women brands that linked the product to their personal needs and desires. Whether in terms of weight loss, beauty, discretion, or sexual allure, the cigarette was positioned to help women attain something more than just sitting back and savoring a smoke.

Technology was another favored subject: cigarette packages featured images of electricity, motors, bicycles, and telephones. Such symbols of the modern world positioned the contents as a parallel advance and suggested that the smoker was modern as well. In Europe, Glückman & Son packaged their Special Telephone brand in a deliciously political design. The box of Russian-style cigarettes wrapped in French rice paper depicts a telephone conversation between Czar Nicholas and Marianne, the French personification of liberty, surrounded by French Art Nouveau swirls and imperial Russian ornaments. Sans-serif typography adds a machine-made touch and the whole package has a transitory quality: the czar would soon be deposed, Russia would change forever, and war would engulf the nations.

War was good for the cigarette industry. Manufacturers on all sides of World War I promoted their products as part of the war effort, and governments requisitioned tobacco as essential rations for their fighting men. Bull Durham's wartime slogan was "When you light up, the Huns will light out," but for American doughboys World War I was really more about Camels, which were distributed by the government in proportion to their popularity as the prewar market leader. Playing picture games with Camel packs became a favorite soldier's pastime. Memories of stealing a moment's peace in the trenches by finding the crouching lion (camel's back), the naked lady (camel's side), or the man with the erection (camel's front leg and shoulder) would translate into brand loyalty once the war was over. Among British soldiers, a pack of Woodbines was the desired tobacco ration, and there was even a legendary cigarette-dispensing priest known as Woodbine Willy. French soldiers preferred the classic blue pack

Special Telephone (ABOVE, TOP)
Glückman & Son, Europe, c. 1910

Cuates (Nonidentical Twins)
(ABOVE, BOTTOM)
Cigarrera Internacional, Mexico,
c. 1930

of their Gauloises, decorated with a winged helmet of Liberty (page 53).

The war spelled the end of Turkish tobacco's prominence for the Allies. Shortages caused partially by the huge wartime demand for tobacco and partially by fighting in Asia Minor (a major cultivation site of Turkish tobacco) interfered with the Turkish tobacco market. After the war nothing could rekindle America's desire for the Turkish brands. Advertisements showing war-toughened soldiers clutching ornate packs of Murads in their fists just didn't work. Slightly more expensive and bearing fussily romantic personas and scenes from a region that was no longer such an appealing mystery, the Egyptian brands now seemed frivolous and, with all their ornamentation, somehow not only unmanly but almost un-American. Germany, on the other hand, retained its taste for, and access to, Turkish tobacco—to this day, brands with Turkish themes like Nil and Senoussi remain popular there.

In the U.S. the look of the new became clear in 1917, when the American Tobacco Company released Lucky Strike (page 7). The pack's graphics consist of a simple red target on a green background, accompanied by two small bits of information—the brand name and a little cursive slogan below it, "They're toasted." The slogan would prove immensely successful: even though all cigarettes are made with toasted, or cured, tobacco, consumers didn't know that, and they were attracted to the promise of mellow flavor. The design's masculine simplicity and the glowing ad copy descriptions of Lucky's "toasting" fit the needs of the postwar years. Homeward-bound doughboys, reaching for a Lucky, would be reminded of the toasty comforts of domestic life.

Chesterfield was redesigned by Liggett & Myers around 1917 to compete with Lucky Strike and marketed as a milder smoke. The Chesterfield graphics epitomize its mellow blend of domestic and Turkish tobaccos (containing far more of the cheaper domestic leaf) by superimposing heraldic elements on an Oriental-looking city that politely fades into the clean white background. Almost 95 percent of the American market in the 1920s would smoke Camels, Chesterfields, or Lucky Strikes. In 1925 Philip Morris launched Marlboro, a revitalized version of its 1908 Marlborough, as a hopeful rival. The new version came in a man's and woman's variety; both packages featured the Philip Morris crest and signature on a white ground, suggesting upscale quality (page 24). The man's cigarette was packaged with "ivory tips," the lady's featured red "beauty tips" to avoid unsightly lipstick stains. An illusionist rip on the woman's package was designed to look as if it revealed the red-tipped cigarettes inside.

Packages in other parts of the world displayed less minimalist sensibilities. In South America two brands from around 1930—Brazil's Andrade y Andrade, a rural peasants' brand, and Chile's La Torre Eiffel, marketed in the city—encapsulate the difference between *el campo* and *la ciudad*. The Brazilian

Chesterfield
Liggett & Myers Tobacco Co.,
U.S.A., 1920s; introduced in
1917

pack features corn-husk-wrapped cigarettes in a paper band decorated with a life-size drawing of a fly (since the wrapper was glued right onto the cigarettes, the smoker got a lungful of glue with each inhale). Marketed as a down-and-dirty brand in villages where most people were illiterate, the pack would have been instantly recognizable, with the fly a clever, wordless joke. The urban La Torre Eiffel, on the other hand, features the Eiffel Tower as never before seen, rising up out of a scrub countryside with the same naive, false realism of Egyptian cigarette packaging from a couple of decades before. The tower, celebrated as a sign of French modernity, is framed in old-fashioned ornament, giving the effect of a souvenir postcard. A U.K. contemporary, the whimsical, slightly macho Black Cat, features the company's mascot, with his tomcat, nocturnal, freedom-loving persona, in an ornate neo-Baroque frame. Black Cat enjoyed high popularity in England, as did John Player's Navy Cut, Gold Flake, and most of all, Wild Woodbine.

Andrade y Andrade
(ABOVE, LEFT)
Andrade y Andrade, Brazil, c. 1930

La Torre Eiffel (ABOVE, RIGHT)
Chile, c. 1930

Many of the brands made by local, lesser companies used graphics to stoke the imagination with imagery instead of words. You don't need to read La Torre Eiffel to know what you're seeing, since by then it was an internationally famous icon of the new century. There was a new swiftness to perception, which manufacturers of both domestic and export brands understood. This faster visual perception developed in tandem with the faster delivery of images from manufacturers and with the need to position a brand instantly, in ever-changing markets. In China, BAT struggled to maintain its grip as national attitudes turned against British imports. In 1925, to circumvent a crippling boycott of its flagship brand, Ruby Queen, the firm renamed it Red Pack. All traces of a connection to monarchic Britain were erased, replaced by a meaningless name designed to suit both traditional Chinese culture, in which red signifies fortune, and China's new political climate. The repositioned brand succeeded in recapturing a market by capturing the spirit of the new times.

Black Cat (BELOW, LEFT)
Carreras, U.K., late 1920s

Washington (BELOW, RIGHT)
Day Hwa Tobacco Co., China, 1920s

Washington cigarettes, manufactured in the same era by China's own Day Hwa Tobacco Company, have a logo spelled out in plain English: by now, certain words functioned as global symbols, and their presence signaled progress and modernity. These were words that weren't so much read as recognized. Day Hwa's package depicts Washington, D.C., as a stylized group of templelike buildings topped by

Capitol-style domes. The scene looks like a printer's interpretation of a barely legible photograph glimpsed in a newspaper. But it was the dream of Washington, not the appearance of it, that was important.

Cleverness and whimsy regained their place in American cigarette packaging when the Great Depression hit. As the Big Three (Reynolds, Lorillard, and ATC) engaged in price hikes and price wars, other brands, known as the ten-centers, slipped into the market with cheaper alternatives and smaller companies resorted to lighthearted gimmicks to stay afloat. Reed Tobacco launched Domino, featuring a smiling flapper who looks like the embodiment of fun (page 79). The Louisville-based Axton-Fisher Company, then the largest independent tobacco company in the world, offered brands whose jocular packaging reflected both the firm's edgy success and the jokester sensibility of its leader, Colonel Woodward Fitch Axton. Its ten-center Twenty Grand, a Turkish-Domestic blend, features a portrait of a spirited but wise-looking racehorse (page 82). Layers of daydreams are conveyed by this package, from the implicit invitation to bet on Twenty Grand and win a bundle to the dreamy sound of that large a sum of money, which would have enabled the winner to escape the rigors of the Depression for good.

Those terrible times seemed to inspire a certain subversiveness. Another Axton-Fisher brand cleverly dodged the tax laws requiring each pack to bear its own tax stamp. Head Play cigarettes were in a package eleven inches tall, ready to be separated into four identical packs of proper size, using the helpful perforations. On each pack, Head Play the racehorse (a real winner of the Kentucky Derby) eyes his coconspirator, the smoker, with an in-the-know expression, framed by a lucky horseshoe.

Axton-Fisher's major brand of the period was the "menthol-cooled" Spud with cork tips. Colonel Axton bought the brand for a reported $90,000 from an eccentric Ohioan, Lloyd "Spud" Hughes, who had figured out how to blend cured tobacco leaves with menthol. Hughes used his profits to indulge his real passion: airplanes. He opened his own airport, entered and staged daring air races, and became known for spectacularly reckless flying. By 1928 (some two years after Axton bought his menthol brand), Hughes had squandered it all and was working at a gas station while he schemed to invent another cigarette, this time blended with the ingredients for a mint julep.

Spuds's giddy typography almost pokes fun at itself. But the cigarette's innovations reflected a new era, when scientific advances were dovetailed into marketing schemes. The word *scientific* became as key to an ad campaign as a movie star's endorsement. Some cigarettes, such as those targeted to women, would play both cards, with a starlet extolling the slimming, healthful virtues of smoking a particular brand. Brown & Williamson got on the scientific bandwagon with their release of Viceroy in 1936. Viceroys featured a cellulose acetate filter that claimed to remove half the smoke in each puff. The company had also launched the mentholated Kool in 1933 to compete with Spud. With its engaging penguin mascot (page 133), Kool would soon surpass the brand it imitated.

The reputed soothing properties of certain ingredients—filters, menthol, glycol instead of glycerin in the case of Philip Morris cigarettes—may have assuaged the public's fears of irritation and toxicity, but they did little to calm the experts. By 1938 a Johns Hopkins researcher had confirmed that smokers had a shorter life expectancy than nonsmokers. A year later a German scientist at the University of Cologne demonstrated an irrefutable link between smoking and lung cancer. *Consumer Reports* began to rate U.S. cigarettes, listing the nicotine content of the top standard brands: Chesterfields had the most and Camels and Lucky Strikes the least, but the difference between them was slim. In just one of the ironies of cigarette smoking history, it was those boys from World War I, their wartime morale boosted by cigarettes that had been airdropped, shipped, mailed, and passed around, who provided scientists with their population of guinea pigs. As lung cancer statistics swelled, the correlation between the disease and smoking were becoming frighteningly clear. A large percentage of war veterans had survived one of history's bloodiest conflicts only to fall to a smoking-related disease.

The years leading up to World War II brought no slowdown of smoking. The exception was Germany, where the growing national abhorrence of ailment and affliction had combined with existing anti-smoking lobbies to produce laws against public smoking in many cities. But in countries from Italy to the Soviet Union, state-run tobacco monopolies used the cigarette pack to promote nationalism and to make money. The Italian tobacco monopoly celebrated Fascism's rise with the late-1920s brand Eja, whose title echoes the exclamation with which crowds hailed Mussolini. The design features a striking black eagle, its wing raised in salute, standing in front of a stylized heraldic lion. A metaphor is at play here: it looks as if the eagle has sunk its talons into the cornice of old, crumbling Rome, having landed there to announce the arrival of the new order.

The Soviet tobacco monopoly released a number of brands

Head Play (OPPOSITE, LEFT)
Axton-Fisher Tobacco Co., U.S.A., 1933

Spud (OPPOSITE, RIGHT)
Axton-Fisher Tobacco Co., U.S.A., mid-1930s; introduced in 1926

Eja
Monopolio dei Tabacchi, Italy, 1928

commemorating the goals and achievements of the Stalinist era, among them the mid-1930s Belomor Canal, named for the massive forced-labor project to connect the White Sea and the Baltic. Despite the tremendous loss of life it caused (up to 700 political prisoners a day) and despite the inconvenient fact that the finished canal was too shallow for the oceangoing ships it was supposed to serve, the brand inspired tremendous pride and loyalty. Still sold in its original form—a short, wide pack containing cardboard tubes half-filled with cheap Makhorka tobacco—the brand remains a national favorite. To the older generation who look back on Stalinist times with nostalgia and scoff at the modern rage for Western brands, Belomor Canals are a symbol of a superior past. To the younger generation, the brand has another draw: the harsh tobacco in the easily emptied cardboard tube can be replaced with marijuana.

In contrast to the cheaply printed Belomor Canals was a Soviet export brand released for promotional use at the 1939 New York world's fair. The Soviet Pavilion cigarette package almost poetically embodies the ideals of the Soviet state. A blue-clad worker stands on a dark blue platform lifting up a bright red star. The star seems to glow, surrounded by a bright light that gradually diffuses, as if evaporating into the smoke-filled air at a triumphant gathering of workers.

An American link between patriotism and cigarettes was made in 1942, when Lucky Strikes were redesigned with a white rather than a green background (page 7). Ad campaigns proudly stated that Luckies had nobly "gone to war," contributing the titanium and bronze required for its green ink to the war effort. The metals, it was claimed, would help make four hundred light tanks, though there was no way to prove it. In reality, all cigarette companies contributed to the war effort by giving up the foil liners in their packages, though none of the others capitalized so brazenly on the marketing opportunity.

Belomor Canal (ABOVE, TOP)
U.S.S.R., 1980s; introduced in 1930s

U.S.S.R. (ABOVE, BOTTOM)
U.S.S.R., 1939

Wartime propaganda packs crossed national borders: the American-made Going Forward was air-dropped and shipped to the Chinese army in 1944 as a gesture of friendship for America's Chinese allies. Adorned with Chinese characters, the pack features a bayonet-wielding soldier, rolling tank, and airplane, all moving in the same direction and all glowing red, as if lit by the glare of

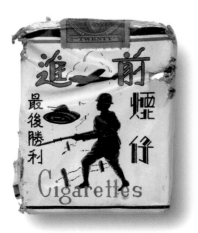

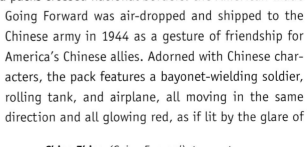

Chien Zhing (Going Forward) (FAR LEFT)
U.S.A., 1944

Hikari (Light) (LEFT)
Japan Imperial Tobacco Company, Japan, 1944

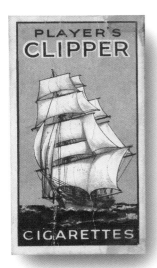

Clipper (FAR LEFT)
John Player & Sons, U.K., 1940

Clipper (LEFT)
Central Tobacco Co., U.S.A., 1940

a mortar-shell blast. A different kind of light shows up on a pack of Hikari ("light" in Japanese), produced at the same time by the Japan Imperial Tobacco Company. The package's one-color printing on poor-quality paper—reflecting Japan's acute wartime shortages—is used to full advantage in the simple but dynamic design. A rising sun, long a symbol of Japan, enters the sky with a light so intense that its rays seem to blast away the darkness, presumably in a metaphor for the radiant power of the Japanese military. The fiery ball might even symbolize a kamikaze plane, exploding in heroic self-sacrifice.

Meaning also shifts in the designs of two cigarette packs, both named Clipper—one from the U.K.'s John Player & Sons, the other from the U.S. Central Tobacco Company. Both glorify the technological might that won wars, but one nation looks back for its confidence while the other looks up. The British design recalls the bygone era when the British navy's grand clipper ships ruled the high seas. The American pack also features the ocean, complete with roiling whitecaps and sailing ships. But the ships are mere wisps on the horizon, and the ocean waves have been stirred up by the turbulence of an immense China Clipper plane soaring overhead.

By midcentury, cigarette package designs had proven that there were infinite ways to sell a paper-wrapped stick of tobacco. In addition to certain themes established back in the wild beginnings at the turn of the century, others emerged. The International Style gave some package designs a sophisticated graphic simplicity. Political changes that affected the cigarette industry itself were reflected in alterations to existing designs. For example, in postwar India, as Britain broke up its empire, industries that had been run by British concerns were taken over by Indians. The circa 1950 brand Rabbit, featuring a white rabbit sitting rather nervously amid tufts of grass, is identified in English on one side, Sanskrit on the other. The extremely poor printing quality—cheap inks on grainy paper, inferior trapping and registration—suggest that it was

Rabbit
India, c. 1950

made on a printing press left behind by the British without instructions or supplies. But somehow the defects add a unique character—it *looks* like a pack of Indian cigarettes. The same could be said for a pack launched in Poland, circa 1950. As Eastern Europe closed its doors to the West, strong local markets started developing. There's a delicate exuberance to the folk-inflected Polish Syrena package design, and the free-form lines of the mermaid-siren suggest an artist's hand. Polish packaging was indeed often designed by fine artists, who were given broad scope in conceiving the designs.

In postwar America, however, tobacco companies were moving away from any association with the handmade or lighthearted, as they gained a sophistication in marketing that would allow them not only to sidestep certain issues but actually take advantage of them. Privately, companies were being compelled to face some indisputable facts about the links between smoking and cancer. Publicly, they developed a new advertising vocabulary of safe-sounding buzzwords and increased their visibility by sponsoring television shows. Just as they had taken advantage of the emergence of commercial radio in the 1920s, cigarette firms now used television to reinforce their presence in popular culture. Lucky Strikes sponsored *Your Hit Parade*; Philip Morris sponsored *I Love Lucy*.

In 1952 Lorillard introduced the elegantly styled Kent cigarettes with claims that Kent's new "Micronite" filter gave smokers the "greatest cigarette protection in cigarette history." The filter maker, Hollingsworth & Vose, insisted on (and got) a full indemnity agreement from Lorillard. The filters, it turned out, were made of asbestos, then considered a miracle fiber but now known to be deadly. Lawsuits would follow a few decades later. Meanwhile, America's cigarette consumption in 1950 was ten cigarettes per capita—more than a pack a day if divided up among adult smokers, who constituted up to 47 percent of the U.S. population. In the same year, a well-publicized *British Medical Journal* study found that heavy smokers were fifty times more likely to develop lung cancer than nonsmokers.

Cigarette manufacturers of the 1950s and 1960s responded to the growing number of lawsuits (in that era, all unsuccessful), the various medical studies coming out, and the attempts at antismoking legislation with a nonchalance matched only by the car industry. As industrial designer Raymond Loewy observed of his redesigns for Lucky Strikes, the new white package had a clean, fresh—ergo, "safe"—look. Looked downright healthful, actually. Couched in visual language that worked too subconsciously to question, packaging was now used to allay any fears of health risks. Japan's 1960 "Hi-lite" king-size filter cigarettes were swathed in ice blue and white, clean as a hospital room. The cool palette implies that filtered cigarettes (a fad Hi-lites introduced to Japan) offer a cool smoke. Other Japanese brands—Peace and Hope, both redesigned in 1960—express a tranquil modernism, in which a dove of peace and an arrow of hope, respectively, may contain a vestige of heraldic symbolism but are mostly about simple purity. In the designs, with their use of restrained, businesslike navy blue and peaceful white, and with decorative elements so simple they seem austere, smokers could perceive a calming message with overtones of workmanlike practicality. Work, after all, would rebuild postwar Japan and keep it healthy. In the U.S., Philip Morris, having acquired Benson & Hedges in the 1950s, introduced Benson & Hedges multifilter menthols in 1969, packaging them in a green-and-white combination that mirrored the colors often used in connection with the ecology movement. A reassuringly scientific-looking illustration on the package of two cross-sections of the charcoal "multifilter" was intended to give smokers a sense that science was working for them. They believed it, for a while.

In some instances, the big companies opted out of the health debate altogether. Having acknowledged to themselves (if not to the public) the addictive nature of nicotine, they counted on the human need to buy another pack even before the old one was empty. The brands that smokers chose seemed to be determined by intangible qualities, from the airy stuff of dreams to personality traits that might be found in certain animals or historical characters. But now certain features, like filters, began to play a role in brand selection. Filters had first been employed in cigarette brands aimed at the women's market. Throughout history, women had been offered fancied-up cigarettes in one form or another, from perfumed Turkish varieties to crimson-tipped Fems and even matchstick-size cigarettes that a woman could, in theory, smoke undetected. But the men would soon choose filtered cigarettes as well, as the success of the new Marlboro proved.

Marlboro's package had been overly fussy, without any one element to catch the eye. In 1955 Philip Morris instructed designer Frank Gianninoto to give it a new, burly appeal. The resulting red-and-white graphic—in which the white bottom half rises into the red upper half like a confident, muscular arrow—reduced the original heraldic crest to a minor element but didn't abandon it entirely. The result obeyed a cardinal rule in brand redesign: don't redesign too much, or you'll lose that all-important factor of familiarity, but redesign enough so that you'll attract a new batch of loyalists.

The new package was bright as a stoplight and could be recognized from yards away; it was instantly identifiable even on a static-snowed television screen. Gianninoto had also given Marlboros a new "flip-top" box, the first structural innovation in years; its crisp shape looked terrific wrapped into the sleeve of an undershirt or tucked in the pocket of a denim jacket. It was visually bold, but still promised those rugged smokers the coveted moment of quiet

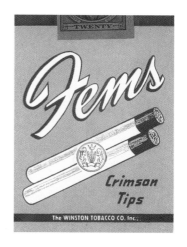

(OPPOSITE, TOP TO BOTTOM)

Syrena (Siren)
Poland, c. 1950

Hi-lite
Japan Tobacco, Japan, 1995;
introduced in 1960

Peace
Japan Tobacco, Japan, 1960s;
introduced in 1920 to commemorate the end of WWI

Hope
Japan Tobacco, Japan, 1960s;
introduced in 1957

Fems (ABOVE, TOP)
Winston Tobacco Co., U.S.A., 1940

Vanity Fair (ABOVE, BOTTOM)
Stephano Brothers, U.S.A., 1956

Marlboro
*Philip Morris & Co., U.S.A., 1925
(right) and 1960 (far right)*

peace that only a cigarette could provide: a perfect combination. To help the campaign along, Philip Morris began to market these cigarettes using the Marlboro Men—first a series of callused working types and then (in response to test marketing) just the cowboy. The cowboy and his Marlboro cigarette became interchangeable icons; one could stand in for the other. In a subtle dismissal of the health debates then raging, Philip Morris sloganeered "Come to where the flavor is." In Marlboro Country, of course, no one got sick. And everyone, everywhere, from India to Asia to Africa to Alaska, wanted to be in that kind of imaginary paradise. Imitators would make the leap from Marlboro's packaging to its cowboy icon, wrapping their brands in denim blue (page 110). The top U.S. brand in 1970 was Winston, another filter brand that based its appeal on flavor. Then, in descending order, were Pall Mall, Marlboro, Salem, and Kool. Within the next nine years, Marlboro would reach the top of the list.

The Surgeon General had ruled that health warning labels had to be on each and every pack beginning in 1966. But the American tobacco industry made sure they were neatly shunted onto a side panel, where they wouldn't spoil the image. The more the industry spent on advertising, the less the dangers of smoking were covered in the press. By the 1970s, cigarettes were the most heavily advertised product in America.

Camel began to search for ways to rebuild its market share in the early 1980s. In order to sell more cigarettes in a saturated market, it would have to appeal to a new generation of smokers. As the decade continued and R. J. Reynolds began developing strategies to increase Camel's sales, other examples of "segment marketing"—targeting a specific group of smokers—began to emerge as well, reflected first and foremost in the packaging. Philip Morris Switzerland targeted the European Gen-X niche with, among other brands, its colorful, punchy Star cigarettes, featuring a graffitied section of the Berlin Wall, faux-Constructivist collages, and other designs. Gen-Xers in both the U.S.

Star
Philip Morris & Co., Switzerland, 1985

and Europe would be courted with a host of gimmicks, as cigarette makers tried to synthesize their complicated view of the world on the front of a cigarette package. Such was the intention of the Black Death package (page 7)—more like an anti-package really, with that grinning skull in a top hat. Irony? Go-to-hell rebelliousness? Punk? Metal? Perhaps it was trying to be all of those at once.

While the U.S. manufacturers would launch apparently less slick, seemingly regional brands at home to counter the growing resistance to "Big Tobacco," their export programs stepped up the promotion of standard brands to more willing markets overseas. The opening of the Japanese market in the 1980s had yielded a number of Japanese brands positioned in direct competition with American brands: Virginia Slims was rivaled by the Japanese Misty, Camel came up against Dean (named for actor James Dean). But anything American, particularly as American as Marlboro, was still considered the ideal. In Russia, India, Thailand, China, Japan, Africa, or anywhere else, American cigarettes were guaranteed to sell.

Buz (ABOVE, LEFT)
Star Tobacco Corp., U.S.A., 1995

Politix (ABOVE, RIGHT)
Moonlight Tobacco Co., U.S.A., 1995

The retro-look cigarettes that American companies released in the 1980s to try to maintain their success at home include American Spirit (page 102), marketed as pure tobacco unsullied by chemicals, in packages marked by a stylized traditional Indian headdress and kitschy, 1950s-linoleum colors. Somehow, the revision seemed more politically correct than the original. The basic premise was that the Indian, a longtime symbol of unspoiled America coopted by the bad, chemical-wielding tobacco companies, was now returned to its rightful place as representative of the pure. Another brand played with the assumption that a cigarette package should look slick. Buz, manufactured by Star Tobacco Corporation, had a minimalist, industrial look reinforced by purposely rough-edged typography. And RJR Nabisco (the conglomerate that R. J. Reynolds had grown into) introduced "micro-smokery" brands such as Politix, attributed to the Moonlight Tobacco Company. In reality, Moonlight Tobacco was just a division of Reynolds. Such brands combining retro design and an irreverent "let's party" attitude were never introduced in dozens of cities at once; to maintain their faux small-company feel, they would appear slowly, starting off in cities like Seattle, New York, or Portland, Oregon, and expanding into the mainstream only if they did well in these test markets.

Karo (Diamond)
Germany, 1998

The retro look also enlivened the East German Karo and F-6, both of which were revived older brands. To an East Germany facing a new future after the collapse of the Berlin Wall, these brands expressed a reassuring link between the past and what lay ahead. Karo's straight, unfussy design fuses a

Uptown
R. J. Reynolds Tobacco Co.,
U.S.A., 1990

Camel Filters
R. J. Reynolds Tobacco Co.,
U.S.A., 1995

Euro-style classicism and slightly Gen-X humor. None of these package designs, from the retro kitsch-hip marketed to Generation X, to the elegant reissues, even to the restrained boldness of the perennially successful Marlboro was inherently controversial.

Controversy came to cigarette packaging when two marketing campaigns revealed carefully targeted appeals that bordered on outright exploitation. Both involved RJR Nabisco, which had been looking for a way not only to revive Camel's market but also to make forays into the urban black segment (which seemed to prefer Kools and Newports). So it began test marketing a brand called Uptown in the inner cities. Uptown came in menthol, and it was designed with a look of ghetto ostentatiousness, involving a lot of gold on a dark background. The unmistakably legible logo was backed by a long black wedge that climbed steeply upward, penetrating the upper region of the package with a sharp point. Aspiration? Sexuality? Was RJR Nabisco trying to distill the dreams of the black male into this design? The Health and Human Services secretary, Louis W. Sullivan, an African American, had his suspicions. He led other black civic leaders in a protest campaign that denounced the company's blatant appeal to black males. In a rash of bad publicity, RJR Nabisco canceled the brand.

It would take ten years to resolve the other RJR Nabisco controversy, over Joe Camel. First conceived for an ad campaign running in adult French magazines, Joe Camel was brought to the U.S. in 1987 as a possible solution to Camel cigarette's flagging sales. The anthropomorphized dromedary was part of the long tradition of using animal personas to add character to brands. But, as redrawn by RJR Nabisco artists, he went much further. An awkward man-camel with a preposterously phallic nose, Joe Camel was cool in spite of himself. He wore a leather jacket or a snazzy white tux, rode motorcycles and speedboats, and got the girls. Most of all he smoked, with a preternaturally studied, sexual ease. He looked like a former nerd who had discovered how to be cool.

Though RJR Nabisco wouldn't admit it, Joe Camel was a perfect icon for teenage boys suffering through the most awkward stage in their lives. Like them, Joe Camel wore his sexuality on his face (taking those World War I picture games about finding naked bodies on the Camel pack to a masterfully airbrushed extreme). And with a cigarette as his constant companion, he oozed confidence. Clearly, the world—and especially the rumpy, stacked women in the ads—loved him. RJR Nabisco then started an enormously successful campaign in which buyers would collect "Camel dollars" and redeem them for all sorts of merchandise, from bags to hats to bicycles, all emblazoned with that sexy mascot. By 1991 RJR's Joe Camel marketing campaign had successfully rejuvenated their classic brand. One study tracked Camel's share of the under-eighteen market between 1987 and 1997: the brand's share of the youth market had soared from 0.5 to 34.8 percent.

The public realized, with a shock, that RJR Nabisco was targeting their children. When a research team found that Joe Camel was as recognizable as Mickey Mouse to preschoolers, the backlash gained momentum. In 1997 the Federal Trade Commission accused RJR Nabisco of using Joe Camel to illegally target under-eighteen youth. And though RJR Nabisco feigned indignation and sued the commission for daring to make such an accusation, they killed the Joe Camel campaign that year. The replacement was a "What You Want" campaign, which claimed to have an adult audience in mind. But to many, that claim was suspect, since the campaign's ads of lissome models in come-get-me poses seemed like a teenager's wet dream.

In the 1990s, lawsuits, legislation, and science finally caught up with the cigarette industry. It was the end of tobacco advertising in Europe; the end, in some states, of smoking even in bars. For the first time, a smoking-related personal injury case was decided in favor of the plaintiff, who was awarded a million and a half from a chastened Lorillard Tobacco. No wonder cigarette package designs were going retro. Perhaps they reminded the addled CEOs of better days.

What, then, is the ideal cigarette package for the millennium? Is there a right way to acknowledge in graphic design the good-bad nature of smoking, while still achieving the yes-no-yes that some consumers confess they give in to as they pass the register and decide they just have to buy another pack of Marlboros, or John Players, or Seven Stars?

Perhaps an Australian pack has unwittingly provided the answer. The brand, unveiled circa 1998, is called Holiday, in keeping with one of smoking's oldest themes—momentary escape through a cigarette break. Originally, the pack featured the following scene over its whole front, now it takes up only two-thirds of the area. The scene is a seascape, an abstracted, sun-bright nautical scene. A sailboat races near the horizon, the red-and-white sails of stylized hobie cats tilt playfully in the foreground, a starry-rayed, childishly rendered sun beams over a stretch of tranquil sand, and the ocean shifts from pale green blue in front to darker green blue in back, conveying a wonderful sense of infinite space and time. And yet.

The top third of the pack has been preempted by a government health warning in stern black type on white. Australia's tobacco lobby must lack the clout of those in the U.S. and U.K. because the warning dominates the pack with its bold statement: Smoking Kills. A perfect juxtaposition, unfussy in every way. And, for once, for the first time, absolutely honest.

Of course, Australian smokers love Holiday, particularly for this new, outrageous irony it bears. And no one can claim they don't know what they're doing.

Holiday
Rothmans, Australia, 1999

Orientalism

The Mystique of the Middle East

THE EAGERNESS OF LATE-NINETEENTH-CENTURY cigarette manufacturers to capture the Turkish tobacco market sent many a designer scrambling to depict a Mideast he'd never seen. "Make it look Egyptian" was a common instruction. At the drawing table, artists conjured up a hodgepodge of Greek, Turkish, Moorish, Egyptian, and even Indian motifs. Their sources included illustrated newspaper accounts of Egyptian archaeological discoveries, museum exhibitions of ancient treasures, and popular compendia featuring ornaments from around the world. Designers copied decorative elements and combined them with exotic characters from moguls to sphinxes, producing implausible but appealing flights of fancy.

Murad, a brand designed by S. Anargyros, was originally launched in 1905. The package features a pensive woman—part Cleopatra, part harem girl, and part exhausted tourist—reclining on an awkward-looking lion throne. This was a common piece of ancient Egyptian furniture, but here the lion's head more closely resembles a complacent domestic tabby's, and its tail springs up like a kitten's. The woman leans against a giant red cushion that looks like either a zinnia or the tailfeathers of a turkey, her hand resting alluringly inside her thigh. Two Anubis figures guard her; behind the trio lurks a sloped structure that looks like a cross between a chimney and a pyramid. In the background burns a many-rayed sun.

On the Hungarian Amen Ra brand a band of made-up hieroglyphs frames the design in a fantastically exuberant parade of squiggles, dashes, stylized birds, dots, and a few open eyes, most of which do not repeat. (Imagine the poor artist struggling to invent authentic-looking hieroglyphics just an hour before the mock-up is due.) Amen Ra, which was introduced after the discovery of King Tuthankhamen's tomb in 1922, features a stylized bird that bears some resemblance to the king's rediscovered treasures. The Sphinx, however, is another story: she looks more like a slightly miffed, pale-skinned artist's model, tired of lying propped up on her elbows on the lumpy couch and uncomfortable in that woolly, v-necked lion suit.

In truth, the Turkish tobacco brands were losing their allure, largely due to World War I. The Middle East had become the enemy of the Allies, no longer a fantasy world of sphinxes and harem girls. When the war made Turkish tobacco unavailable to American and British markets, domestic manufacturers stepped up their promotion of cigarettes largely made of Virginia tobacco. The artifice involved in conjuring up a fantasy had a built-in shelf life; when reality hit, the fantasy expired.

Memphis (ABOVE)
Brazil, 1930s

Natural (BELOW)
Schinasi Brothers, U.S.A., 1907

Mecca (OPPOSITE)
S. Anargyros & Co., U.S.A., 1910; introduced in 1891

Murad (ABOVE)
Successors to S. Anargyros & Co.,
U.S.A., 1930s; introduced in 1905

Reliquia (Relics) (FAR LEFT)
Cia. Lopes, Brazil, 1930s

Cairo (LEFT)
Cia. Chilena de Tabacos, Chile, 1910s

Espinge (The Sphinx) (OPPOSITE, TOP LEFT)
Tabacalera de Nicaragua, Nicaragua,
1939

Amen Ra (OPPOSITE, BOTTOM)
Arav & Co., Hungary, 1925

Pyramid *(ABOVE)*
ICI, U.S.A., 1995

This contemporary American brand is manufactured by and for prison inmates: it is the correctional institution's counterpart of Camel. But the imagery has a slightly cruel twist when one considers the purpose of the structures it's named after: the pyramids, after all, were giant tombs. Once sealed up, they were inescapable, much like a prisoner's cell.

Kirli *(ABOVE)*
Germany, 1930s

Turkish Special *(BELOW)*
G. A. Georgopulo & Co., U.S.A., 1949

Fatima *(ABOVE)*
Liggett & Myers Tobacco Co., U.S.A., 1945; introduced in
1887, best-selling Turkish brand in U.S.A. by about 1910

Turkey Red *(OPPOSITE)*
S. Anargyros & Co., U.S.A., 1905

Behold every man's version of Oriental exotica, circa 1905: a
European beauty in "Turkish" garb: part harem girl, part prostitute.
Bathed in red light, she displays a package of Turkey Reds that reads
"Come to stay," a come-hither slogan of the day. Since little was
understood about harems at the turn of the century, artists often
conceived of them as brothels, fussed up with Oriental touches—
veiled and beaded houses of sin. In 1905 cigarette manufacturers
were also trying to shed the association that cigarettes had with
femininity and were creating packages that would play to male fantasy. To add to the sense of the exotic, two fezzes, emblazoned with
Turkish symbols and glowing as if they had lightbulbs inside, float
like lanterns on either side of the beauty's head.

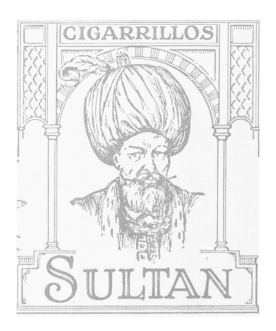

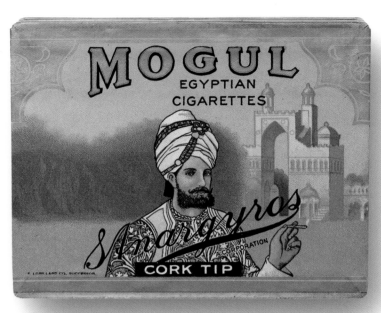

Sultan (ABOVE, LEFT)
Tabacalera Hondureña, Honduras, 1940s

Mogul (ABOVE, RIGHT)
P. Lorillard Tobacco Co., U.S.A., 1939;
introduced by S. Anargyros in 1892

Tamerlane (LEFT)
Albert Baker & Co., U.K., 1900s

Omar (BELOW)
American Tobacco Co., U.S.A., 1937;
introduced in 1902

Fez (OPPOSITE)
Butler & Butler, U.S.A., 1910

SALOME

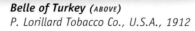

Salome Ideal (OPPOSITE)
Rosedor Cigarette Co., U.S.A., 1924

Belle of Turkey (ABOVE)
P. Lorillard Tobacco Co., U.S.A., 1912

Cleopatra (ABOVE)
Egypt, 1993

Helmar

P. Lorillard Tobacco Co., U.S.A., 1920s; introduced in 1907

In 1907, in an attempt to capture more of the early-century appetite for Turkish cigarettes, S. Anargyros revised its Ramleh brand by reversing the title's letters into the more mellifluous Helmar. The ornamentation on the package is unusual for its detail and may have been copied straight out of a book of ready-made decorations. The standing sarcophagi feature strange, double-antennae headgear, as if the artist had misinterpreted the role of the ancient cobra-shaped head covering.
In 1919 Lorillard unsuccessfully tried to remarket Helmar as a woman's brand.

MEDIUM

The Lure of the Sea
Sailors, Ships, and Smokes

ONE WAY OR ANOTHER, tobacco has always been linked to the sea—sailors smoked it, sailing ships transported it. Cigarette packaging, particularly from the 1870s to 1930s, often capitalized on the heroism and adventure associated with maritime trade and the navy. To the landlubber with dreams of ocean-going freedom, the seafaring life held tremendous allure.

Redford's All's Well of the 1910s features a giant steamer crossing the sea, signal flags strung along its wires with the "All's Well" pattern riding the breeze ahead of two massive smokestacks. The scene of safe waters kept free of enemies by this powerful ship reflects the sense of pride England felt for its navy. In 1912, when the Titanic sunk and the world witnessed a tragedy of legendary proportions, survivors recalled how men had stood on deck in their tuxedos, calmly awaiting their fate with a final cigarette. That image forged a permanent link between stoicism and smoking.

Some package designs commemorate specific moments in nautical history: the English firm Carreras exported its Corvette brand to Canada in the 1940s, immortalizing the Corvette boats that were escorting convoys of merchant ships through the embattled Atlantic of World War II. Far from glamorous, Corvettes carried eighty to ninety men on a crowded, wet, pitching voyage; these 900-tonners were known for their tendency to roll in the slightest chop. But the sailors manning the Corvettes were the pride of Canada: without them, the North American and British merchant ships would not have made it through.

The Japanese Tobacco Monopoly's Mikasa brand pays respect to the country's powerfully built battleships. The package features a giant ship crossing near the horizon, graced by a flag of the rising sun whose red-and-white pattern pops against the murky browns and greens of the scene. Some fifty years later, China immortalized its new economic boom with the Shang You (Sailing Upstream) brand, featuring a gleaming cargo ship muscling through a vividly red sea.

Still other packages pay homage to mercantile conquest and success: a 1990 design of the Monopoli di Stato Italia's classic Esportazione depicts a historic sailing ship, perhaps a frigate or a pirate's two-master. Czechoslovakia's Sparta, a brand still on the market, features an ancient Greek vessel with sinewy, minnowlike lines: look once, it's a boat, look again, it's a fish. The choice of color on both designs—from the Italian brand's green and black to the Czech brand's red, white, and blue—underscores the simplified, silhouetted renderings. As associations of power and modernity shifted from sea to air, then from air to technology and space, there was no longer a need for such realistic, vividly rendered nautical images.

Corvette (ABOVE, TOP)
Carreras, U.K. export to Canada, 1940s

Shang You (Sailing Upstream)
(ABOVE, BOTTOM)
Ningbo Cigarette Factory, China, 1985

Premier's Navy Cut (DETAIL
OPPOSITE, SEE PAGE 40)
Premier Tobacco Co., U.K., 1930s

Premier's Navy Cut (ABOVE)
Premier Tobacco Co., U.K., 1930s

Mikasa (RIGHT)
*Japanese Tobacco Monopoly,
Japan, 1930s*

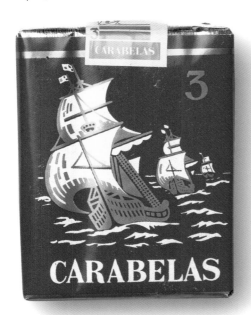

3 Carabelas (ABOVE)
Tabacalera, Spain, 1950s

Sparta (ABOVE)
Czechoslovakia, 1996

Esportazione (ABOVE)
Monopoli di Stato Italia, Italy, 1990

All's Well (OPPOSITE, TOP RIGHT)
Redford & Co., U.K., 1910s

Anchor (OPPOSITE, BOTTOM RIGHT)
Trinidad, 1928

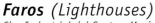

Faros (Lighthouses)
Cia. Industrial del Centro, Mexico, 1920s

The package design of the 1920s Mexican brand Faros (Lighthouses) reads like a scenic painting with metaphorical overtones. A long swath of perspective is compressed onto a small surface, from the lighthouse in the background to the man smoking in the foreground. Early-twentieth-century Latin American cigarette packaging sometimes used unlikely metaphors to communicate the advantages of smoking a cigarette. The brightly lit cylinder of the lighthouse is quietly paralleled by the man's freshly lit cigarette, as if both offer safe harbor for those passing through the night.

Player's Navy Cut
John Player & Sons, U.K., 1940s; introduced as cigarettes 1900

The Player's brand of cigarette, introduced in 1900, bears the likeness of a sailor named Thomas Huntley Wood, who had manned the HMS Edinburgh in the 1880s; his likeness graced pipe tobacco as early as 1883. His visage and surroundings received occasional modifications over the years, and by the 1940s version pictured here, many errors had crept in: the sailor's cap lacks the official "HMS" on its brim, and the flags on the two ships on the horizon fly in opposite directions, as if the sea were divided by opposing winds.

The cigarettes were long popular in England. "Navy cut" refers to an old Royal Navy practice of buying whole leaves of tobacco that sailors would then wind into ropes. To get enough tobacco for a cigarette, a sailor would simply cut a piece off the end of the roll.

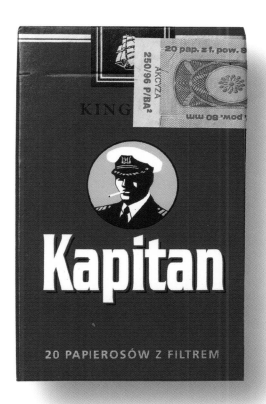

19 Cigaretten

PANAMA

Die EG Gesundheitsminister:
RAUCHEN GEFÄHRDET DIE GESUNDHEIT

Snob Appeal
Trappings of Status and Wealth

CIGARETTE MANUFACTURERS HAVE CATERED to the universal yearning for money and privilege by covering certain brands with heraldry and royal references. Decked out in ritzy gold crests or silver signets, a cigarette package becomes an accessory, offering its owner a cardboard-thin veneer of class. Rivalo, introduced in 1935 by Puerto Rico Tobacco, features an initial R with the foppish swoop of a handlebar moustache. A majestic gold crown within a filigreed frame floats on a woodgrain background.

In contrast, the postwar Japanese Pearl brand features a simple circle, nestled inside a stylized open shell. Wealth here is conveyed by restrained elegance, calculated to appeal to a culture newly crazy about streamlined modern design. That minimalist approach wouldn't have the same appeal in, say, South America. Copas, an Ecuadorian brand contemporary with Pearl, displays the *lotería* card for wealth and good fortune, which is anything but minimalist; the trophy is so vibrant that it seems to have muscle and heart.

Throughout the history of cigarette packaging, obvious references have been made to the superior value of particular brands. P. Lorillard's Old Gold, a classic brand from the 1920s, had a market life that extended for decades. Beneath a jumble of gold coins—or medals—rests the proud slogan, "The Treasure of Them All." To bolster its claim, Lorillard enacted widely publicized blindfold tests that set their brand apart and used testimonials to exalt the brand far above the crowd. As advertising techniques and marketing campaigns became more sophisticated and consumers (particularly in the U.S. and Europe) more jaded, some manufacturers resorted to licensing names that already stood for immeasurable wealth and quality, from Cartier and Harrod's to Rothschilds. The latter, packaged by G. A. Georgopulo in the late 1990s, has the color of an old oxblood leather cigarette case or a millionaire's swanky flask, positioning the cigarettes as a de rigueur accompaniment to expensive brandy. The stance is a throwback to the early days of high-end cigarette marketing, when manufacturers presented their products as modern alternatives to the traditional smoke of luxury, the cigar.

In certain cultures a design that embraces status or wealth takes on a marked poignancy, as in the Cambodia of the 1990s, which is still one of the poorest nations in the world. Viniton Tobacco's brand Luxury, marketed in Cambodia, bears the brand name on the flip-top in elegant cursive; beneath it is a graphic in red and gold, colors that signify strength and prosperity in Cambodian tradition. The brand is most popular in the cities, among the vast ranks of the barely working class and the unemployed.

Essex (ABOVE)
Brazil, 1930s

Luxury (BELOW)
*Viniton Tobacco Company,
Cambodia, 1998*

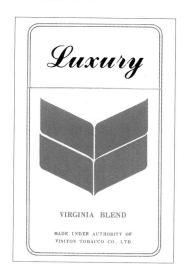

Rivalo (OPPOSITE)
Puerto Rico Tobacco Corp., Puerto Rico, 1944; introduced in 1935

Marlboro
Philip Morris & Co., U.S.A., 1960

The name does trace back to a royal personage, but it's a misconception that Marlboro cigarettes are named after the Duke of Marlborough. In fact, the cigarette was named after Marlborough Street in London—the location of the Philip Morris factory. In 1902 Philip Morris set up shop in New York to bring the Marlborough brand to American markets. When the manufacturer relaunched the cigarette for the women's market in 1924, the "-ugh" in the name was excised, and the brand gained a breezy slogan. According to the advertisements, Marlboros were "as mild as May." A redesign in the 1950s turned it into the boldly masculine, clear-as-a-stop-sign package we know today.

Cartier (*RIGHT*)
Philip Morris & Co., U.S.A., 1991

Rothschilds (*FAR RIGHT*)
G. A. Georgopulo & Co., U.S.A., 1998; introduced in 1980

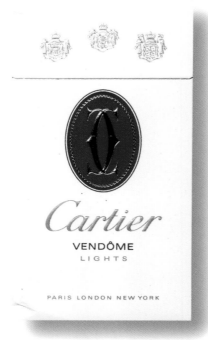

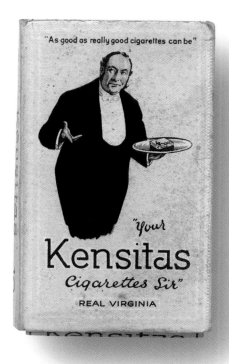

(CLOCKWISE FROM LEFT)

Kensitas
J. Wix & Sons, U.K., 1940s

Lyricos
Brazil, 1930s

Avenida Chic
Brazil, 1930s

Tophat
Michiels Niel, Belgium, 1930s

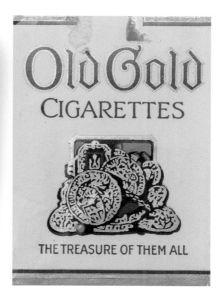

Gold Flake (BELOW)
W. D. & H. O. Wills, U.K., 1930s

Gold Flake referred to the amber tones found in Virginia Bright tobacco, which cures to a golden yellow. It also suggests that this highly sought after, mellower smoke was as valuable as gold. There were many brands called Gold Flake, all of which feature yellow packages trimmed with gold and sometimes have coins and medals added to convey the effect of wealth. W. D. & H. O. Wills's version, adorned with "prize medal no. 62," was the best known.

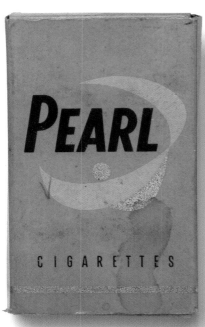

Copas (Trophies) (OPPOSITE)
Cia Ecuatoriana de Tabacos, Ecuador, 1930s

Opal (ABOVE, TOP LEFT)
Bulgartabac, Bulgaria, 1980

Old Gold (ABOVE, TOP RIGHT)
P. Lorillard Tobacco Co., U.S.A., 1920s introduced 1884

Pearl (ABOVE, BOTTOM)
Japanese Tobacco Monopoly, Japan, 1950s

(CLOCKWISE FROM LEFT)

Raja
P. T. Banjuintan, Indonesia,
late 1960s

Prince
House of Prince,
Sweden, 1996

Prince de Monaco
E. D. Laurens, United Arab
Republic, 1940s

La Marquise
Butler & Butler, U.S.A.,
1910s; introduced in 1904

Peter I
Russia, 1995

Three Kings
American Tobacco Co.,
U.S.A., 1938

Monarchs (OPPOSITE)
El Aguil, Mexico, 1940s

Politics & Propaganda
Patriotism by the Pack

PATRIOTISM AND POLITICS have found an effective soapbox in cigarette packaging, whether in the form of nationalist agendas, wartime propaganda, or electioneering. Certain packs play national variations on larger patriotic themes, with their succinct purposefulness adding an ironic layer of posterity to disposable goods. Wartime brands infuse such patriotic themes with a sense of urgency intended to elicit immediate reactions in the smoker-citizens.

During World War II the French Gauloises, featuring the winged helmet of the ancient Gaul warriors, communicated an austere pride. Under German occupation, the French fiercely guarded their increasingly rare brand; a packet of Gauloises became a subversive sign of resistance. Britain's James Carlton introduced V cigarettes for wartime, part of the larger Allied propaganda effort to boost morale during Occupation. The Allies' Victory campaign had as its theme song the first four notes of Beethoven's Fifth Symphony, which sang out the dot-dot-dot-dah melody of the Morse code signal for the letter *V*. Europeans in occupied territory would sing the theme to annoy German soldiers. Before the U.S. entered the war, Britain was the only unoccupied country left to fight the Axis; it bore up to this responsibility in a range of ways, including BBC broadcasts that beamed the V theme to occupied territories. The cigarette package, in wartime-shortage colors, features a bold, straightforward V on a background whose busy, regular pattern could signify radio waves or the endless dots and dashes of Morse code feeding information across enemy lines. In this case, smoking a pack of V's seemed like a contribution to the war effort.

The Japanese Tobacco Monopoly's Kanshi (Golden Eagle) was included in the army's rations. Its early 1940s packaging features two stylized flags of the rising sun and an eagle flying above that seems to be sighting its distant prey. The bird's powerful wings hold it steady in midair, suggesting the skill and courage of a Japanese pilot, and the strength and maneuverability of a Japanese plane. Completing the reference are fine lines radiating from the eagle, suggesting the sight lines on an airplane's instrument panel.

Frankly nationalist, the Chinese May Day brand borrowed from no other nation, making use of the vivid crimson associated with the Chinese Cultural Revolution. May Day's triumphant farming couple exults in their superior harvest by raising their wheat in the air and giving a people's salute; factories work away in the background, as if their industrial success were based on the success of agriculture. All of this illustrates the era's party line with the cheerful clarity of a primer.

Otori Wings *(ABOVE)*
Japanese Tobacco Monopoly, Japan, 1943

Gauloises *(BELOW)*
SEITA, France, 1940; introduced in 1910

Wuyi Xiangyan *(May Day)*
(OPPOSITE)
Gouying Ningbo, China, 1970s

STEVENSON
for PRESIDENT

STEVENSON
for PRESIDENT

STEVENSON
FOR
PRESIDENT
CIGARETTES

Tobacco Blending
Corporation
Louisville 1, Ky.

for PRESIDENT

FACTORY No. 10, DISTRICT OF KENTUCKY

NOTICE: THE MANUFACTURER OF THE CIGARETTES HEREIN CONTAINED HAS COMPLIED WITH ALL REQUIREMENTS OF LAW. EVERY PERSON IS CAUTIONED NOT TO USE EITHER THIS PACKAGE FOR CIGARETTES AGAIN, OR THE STAMP THEREON AGAIN, NOR TO REMOVE THE CONTENTS OF THIS PACKAGE WITHOUT DESTROYING SAID STAMP. UNDER THE PENALTIES PROVIDED BY LAW IN SUCH CASES.

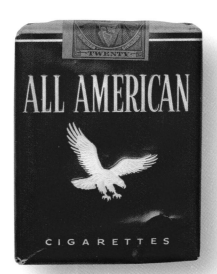

ALL AMERICAN

CIGARETTES

Cigarros
TIO SAM
SEM NICOTINA

20 CLASS A CIGARETTES

(CLOCKWISE FROM LEFT)

Seal of the President of the United States
White House gift, U.S.A., 1980s

Tio Sam
Brazil, 1930s

All American
Axton-Fisher Tobacco Co., U.S.A., 1941

Stevenson for President
Tobacco Blending Corp., U.S.A., 1952

I Like Ike *(OPPOSITE)*
Tobacco Blending Corp., U.S.A., 1952

"I LIKE IKE"

Bandera Roja (Red Flag) (*ABOVE*)
Luis Bigott, Venezuela, 1930s

Yankee (*ABOVE*)
Joseph Licari, Malta,
1940s

Glory (*ABOVE, RIGHT*)
Tobacco Alternatives,
U.S.A., 1996

Araraquara (*RIGHT*)
Brazil, 1930s

B-29
Maria Guizon, Philippines, 1940s

Maria Guizon's B-29 brand commemorates the recapture
of Manila Bay from the Japanese by Allied forces in 1945.
The American B-29 bombers used in the campaign became
a symbol of Yankee prowess and modern military skill. The
plane on this pack, carefully rendered by the artist, soars
across the sky, carrying a payload of twenty cigarettes in
its hold.

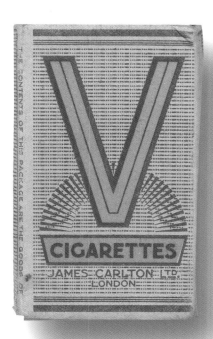

Armeiski *(Armies)* *(BELOW)*
U.S.S.R., 1980

Armored Force *(RIGHT)*
Manufactured for army divisions,
U.S.A., 1942

Pride *(ABOVE)*
Japanese Tobacco Monopoly, Japan,
1941

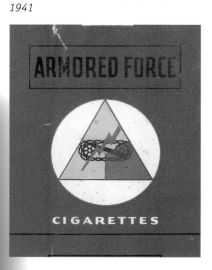

V *(ABOVE, TOP)*
James Carlton, U.K., 1940s

Kanshi *(Golden Eagle)* *(ABOVE, BOTTOM)*
Japanese Tobacco Monopoly, Japan,
1942

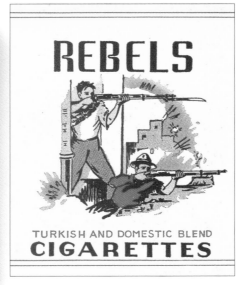

Patriotas *(LEFT)*
El Buen Tono, Mexico, 1940s

Hero and Steed *(ABOVE)*
Hwa Shano Tobacco Co., China, 1930s

Cannon *(BELOW, LEFT)*
Drummond Tobacco Co., U.S.A., 1898

Rebels *(BELOW, RIGHT)*
Axton-Fisher Tobacco Co., U.S.A., 1937

Bogatiri (Heroes) *(OPPOSITE)*
Yava, U.S.S.R., 1948

The Soviet Heroes brand from 1948 features a trio of Tartars on horseback, long symbols of Russia's warrior heritage. The artist took liberties: the riders are all the same size, but not the horses. The central black steed is a giant compared to the pony-size mount on the right, though there is a certain realism in the way each horse has its attention focused in a different direction. The riders, however, are all looking west, as if ready to defend Russia from Western invasion at the onset of the Cold War.

БОГАТЫРИ

Nationals (ABOVE)
Frishmuth Brothers & Co., U.S.A., 1925

Parliament (ABOVE)
Benson & Hedges, Canada, 1940s

Yankee Girl (ABOVE)
Daniel Scotten & Co., U.S.A., 1930s

Nacionales (Nationals) (OPPOSITE)
Fabrica Nacional de Tobacos, Chile,
1890s

Independiente (ABOVE)
Argentina, 1930s

Republicana (ABOVE)
Bolivia, 1995

Fast Forward

Packaging Progress

ICONS OF MODERN LIFE serve their purpose well on cigarette packaging. Brands have been named after fast cars, planes, and spaceships, as well as modern conveniences and other less glamorous features of contemporary life. Traffic lights, for example, make a good metaphor for a cigarette break: stop and have a cigarette, but don't linger too long.

Other designs convey modern achievements on an even grander scale. China's Lü Zhou (Green Oasis), still on the market, features a power plant benignly situated between a sheep's meadow and a mountain range. A row of poplar trees leads the eye right down the country road to this great sign of progress. The Soviet Intourist brand of the 1950s, a souvenir pack available to visitors and tourists, embodies progress: the plane motors sturdily over the long stretch of a man-made, red-flagged dam, signaling triumph over the elements of both air and water.

In some cases, a brand is named after an innovation that is so new that just the word alone conveys excitement. The new invention's functions may be telegraphed through the design, as with the Radio brand manufactured by Mexico's El Buen Tono in the early 1920s. The frame around the brand name is

Zipper (DETAIL, SEE PAGE 70)
Brown & Williamson Tobacco Corp., U.S.A., 1940

shaped like a flying bat, as if to show that invisible radio signals can travel the night as swiftly and silently as bats.

A graphic link is made between cigarettes and other modern objects on a 1930s brand exported from England to Malaysia. The design for the Torchlight pack features a flashlight, barely larger than a life-size cigarette, casting a radiating beam through the standing letters of the brand name. The beam is so bright it obliterates shadow. A sense of security is conveyed here: in a pinch, a Torchlight cigarette will light the way.

As the century progressed, speed would most clearly embody progress, whether on land, in the air, or in space. The American brand Zipper, introduced in 1940, shows a cigarette-shaped car racing across the package, trailing dust and vapor. Brands taking to the air included R. & J. Hill's Air Mail brand of the 1930s, sold in England, and the Bulgarian TU-134 brand of the mid-1980s. Both convey the tremendous airborne power of a massive plane. The former uses vapor trails and a dramatically lit descent above the mountains, while the latter features a plane ascending at an impossibly steep angle. Both designs convey an undeniable message: as the modern machine surges forward, we are thrust forward as well.

Lü Zhou (Green Oasis) **(ABOVE)**
Guo Ying Jaikou, China, 1980

Scissors (ABOVE, LEFT)
Successors to W. D. & H. O.
Wills, Pakistan, 1950s

Torchlight (ABOVE, RIGHT)
Gallaher, U.K. export to
Malaysia, 1930s

Pompa (Hand Pump)
(RIGHT)
P. T. Banjuintan,
Indonesia, 1960s

Icebox (FAR RIGHT)
Moonlight Tobacco Co.,
U.S.A., 1995

Key *(ABOVE, LEFT)*
Cope Brothers & Co.,
U.K., 1930s

Radio *(ABOVE, RIGHT)*
El Buen Tono, Mexico,
1923

Cine *(RIGHT)*
Brazil, 1930s

Intourist (*ABOVE*)
TAT, U.S.S.R., 1950s

Airline (*RIGHT*)
Reed Tobacco Co., U.S.A., 1941

(*OPPOSITE, CLOCKWISE FROM BOTTOM*)

Daily Mail
Consolidated Tobacco, Canada, 1950s

TU-134
Manufactured for distribution by
Aeroflot, Bulgaria, 1980s

Alas (*Wings*)
Cigarerala Moderna, Mexico, 1930s

Air Mail
R. & J. Hill, U.K., 1930s

АЭРОФЛОТ

OFFERED BY

TU-134

FILTER CIGARETTES

ALAS

AIR MAIL

GOLDEN HONEYDEW

CIGARETTES

DAILY MAIL

FILTER TIP

CIGARETTES

EXTRA MILD

Sputnik
Yava, U.S.S.R., 1965

Novaya Planeta (New Planet)
(*ABOVE*)
TFK, U.S.S.R., 1958

Cosmos (*BELOW*)
U.S.S.R., 1981

Apollo-Soyuz (*RIGHT*)
Yava/Philip Morris & Co. joint
venture, U.S.S.R./U.S.A., 1975

The Soviet Space Packs

*The Soviet Union immortalized its much-heralded
space program with a host of brands. Interestingly,
each package reflects the program's morale at the
time. The intensely colored New Planet of 1958, introduced at a time of high hopes for the new space program, offers a brightly optimistic vision. Manufactured
in the state tobacco monopoly's Leningrad factory,
the high-end brand was intended for foreign visitors
and dignitaries. The more soberly composed Apollo-
Soyuz brand of 1975 was a joint venture by Philip
Morris and the U.S.S.R.'s Yava, commemorating the
Soviet-American dual venture in space. The package's austerity confines a two-stage rocket to a tiny
universe, like a fish in a bowl. The 1981 Cosmos
brand, introduced at a time when the space program
was deteriorating, offers an abstraction that commemorates the untarnished ideal of the space program more than the then-crumbling reality.*

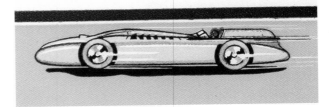

Jeep *(ABOVE, LEFT)*
R. L. Swain Tobacco Co., U.S.A.,
1941

Zipper *(ABOVE, RIGHT)*
Brown & Williamson Tobacco
Corp., U.S.A., 1940

Motor *(OPPOSITE)*
BAT, U.S.A. export, 1900s;
introduced in 1897

*Launched by American Tobacco
in 1897, Motor was exported by
British American Tobacco in the
early 1900s. The package records
what must have been a common
sight at the turn of the century:
a spindly-wheeled motorcar
passing a horse-drawn carriage
on a country road. Here the
relationship between old and new
also expresses the aspirations of
the manufacturer. As one of the
first mass-produced exports
available to any consumer with
the money to buy it, Motor would
enable BAT to overtake any
competition swiftly, particularly
overseas.*

Stop *(ABOVE)*
Monopoli di Stato, Italy, 1950s

Go *(RIGHT)*
Brown & Williamson Tobacco
Corp., U.S.A., 1940; introduced
in 1920

"1897"

MOTOR

VIRGINIA

CIGARETTES

Manufactured by

MOHANLAL HARGO

JABALPUR-INDIA

The Good Life
Marketing Pleasure in a Box

CIGARETTES HAVE ALWAYS EMBODIED PLEASURE. Package designers have long been instructed to sell cigarettes by linking them to happiness, fun, desire, and health. Some of their efforts have become nostalgic with the passing of time, such as the Depression-era Dream Castle, produced by Dream Castle Tobacco in San Francisco, and Pinkerton Tobacco's Sunshine. Others convey a rakish exuberance. The British Passing Show, appeared on both at-home and export packages. The design, featuring a top-hatted bon vivant with florid nose and monocle, conjures up the transient pleasures of a traveling carnival or makeshift cinema. Exported to India, the package with its yellow, gold, and pink coloration would have blended in nicely with the popular Indian palette. Another package, manufactured and sold in India some forty years later, is printed with a photograph of a man lost in thought by a waterfall, as if the cigarette is no longer a novelty in India but a healthy break from the strains of modern life.

Just as scenes of nature have been used on cigarette packs to deflect any health-related fears, so, too, have depictions of athletes or sports been put to use. A Russian-made pack of high-end cigarettes marketed for tourists in Mongolia, Bortsi (Fighters), depicts an open-air traditional match between wrestlers who embody vigor and health. Raul Garcia, a Florida manufacturer, designed La Rumbera (one of its Havana cigarettes of the early 1940s) with a flurry of shiny gold medals surrounding a vivacious dancer. The brand, made from tobacco grown in Cuba, was most likely exported right back to Havana. The meaning of its slogan, "The Cigarette of Tomorrow," shifts depending on the point of view. On the one hand, the medals attest to modern industrial success, since medals were often given out at industrial and trade expositions. On the other hand, perhaps this brand would give the smoker enough energy to dance the rhumba all night long and into tomorrow.

The old link connecting cigarettes to health has been severed, but the connection between cigarettes and good times is still strong. A vibrant example is found in the wild graphics of Club, a 1990s brand manufactured by the Monopoli di Stato Italia. The package depicts life as a wacky chess match, so full of energy that the pieces and board seem ready to jump off the pack. Beneath such kinetic graphics, the health warning is practically invisible.

Dream Castle (ABOVE)
Dream Castle Tobacco Co.,
U.S.A., 1936

Passing Show (BELOW)
Carreras, U.K., 1950s

Mohanlal Hargovinddas
(OPPOSITE)
India, 1998

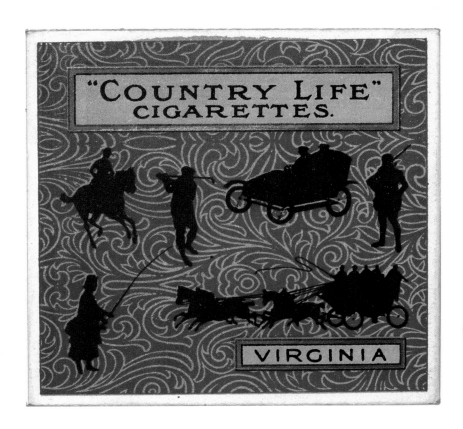

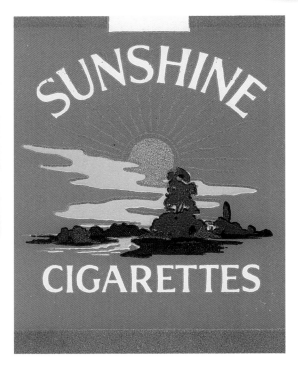

Sunshine
Pinkerton Tobacco Co.,
U.S.A., late 1930s

Horizon
W. D. & H. O. Wills,
Australia, 1998

Country Life
John Player & Sons,
U.K., 1930s

Holiday Kings
Larus & Brothers Co.,
U.S.A., 1955;
introduced in 1948

Habaneros
(Havanans) (OPPOSITE)
El Buen Tono, Mexico,
1910s

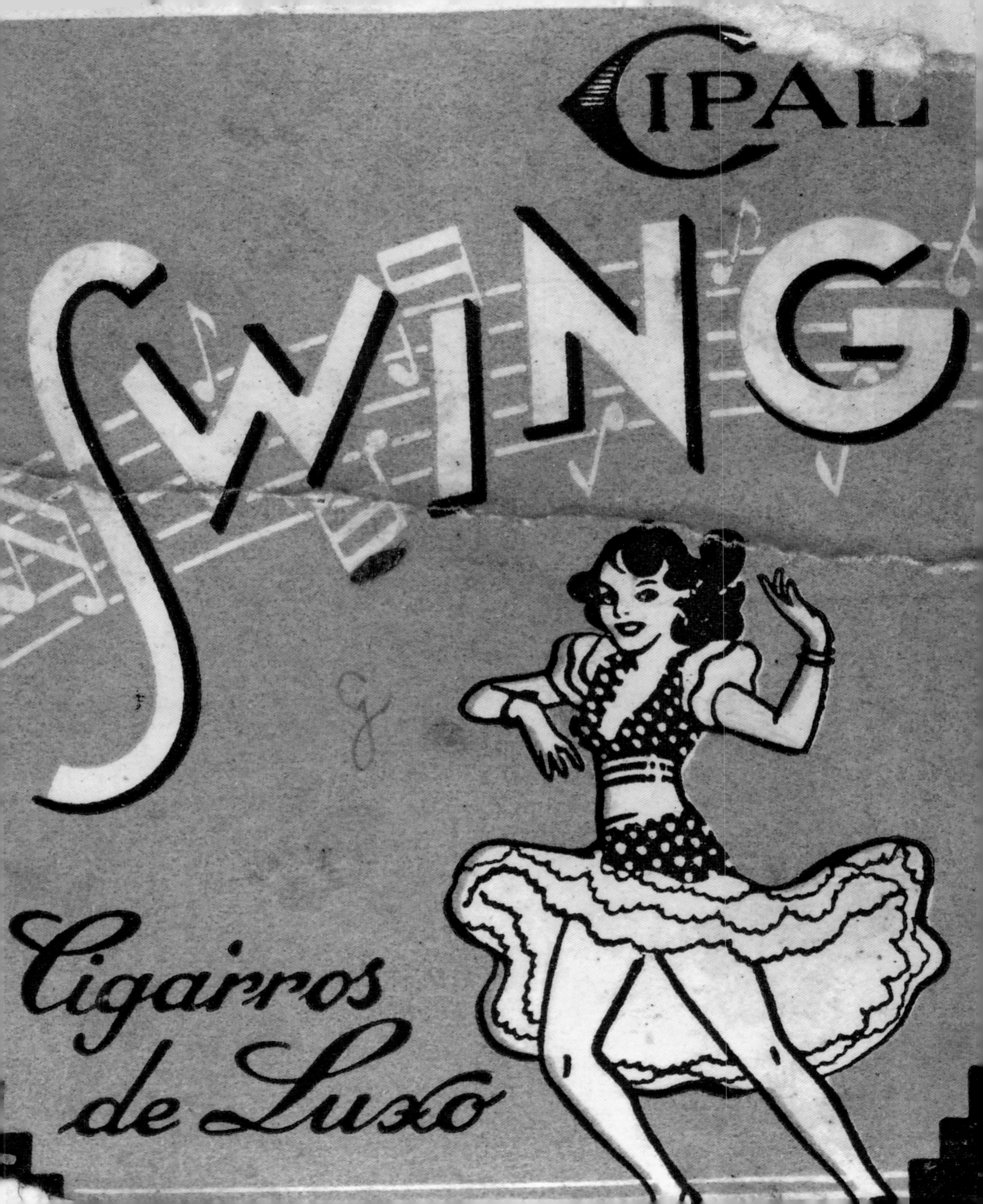
CIPAL
SWING
Cigarros
de Luxo

Swing (*OPPOSITE*)
Brazil, 1930s

Tambor (*RIGHT*)
Tabacalera Istmeña, Panama, 1950s

Sitar (*FAR RIGHT*)
Jupiter Tobacco Co., India, 1950s

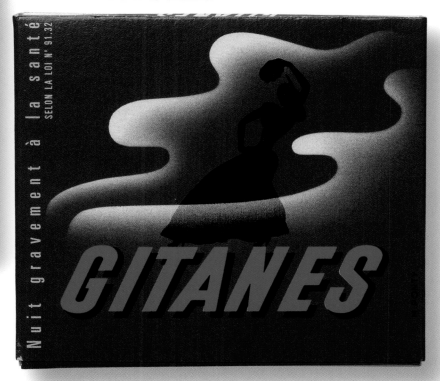

Kuta (*Dancer*) (*LEFT, TOP*)
Indonesia, 1998

La Rumbera (*Rhumba*) (*LEFT*)
Raul Garcia y Cia., U.S.A., 1940s

Gitanes (*Gypsies*) (*ABOVE*)
*SEITA, France, 1998; introduced in 1910,
redesigned by M. Ponty in 1943*

The Good Life **77**

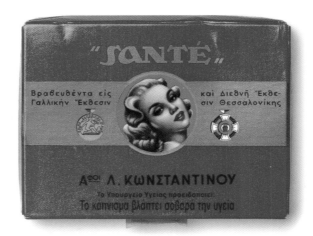

Dukat *(ABOVE, LEFT)*
U.S.S.R., 1950s

Martini *(ABOVE, RIGHT)*
Axton-Fisher Tobacco Co., U.S.A.,
1936

Santé *(Health)* *(RIGHT)*
Greece, 1997

Domino (RIGHT)
*Reed Tobacco Co., U.S.A., 1930s;
introduced in 1933*

Club (BELOW, TOP)
Monopoli di Stato Italia, Italy, 1990

Darts (BELOW, BOTTOM)
Gallaher, U.K., 1940

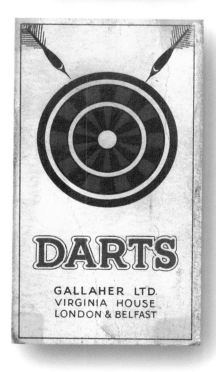

Full House (ABOVE)
*Brown & Williamson Tobacco
Corp., U.S.A., 1928*

Loterico (ABOVE)
Brazil, 1930s

K-O (ABOVE)
La Industrial de Tabacos, Chile, 1910s

The Chilean 1910 brand K-O, named for the American slang for "knock-out," features a design embodying the excitement and violence of a Saturday night prizefight. The dramatic scene depicts a boxing round that has peaked with a punch so severe that it propelled the fighter onto the ropes. The dizzying impact is conveyed by a multirayed sun that bursts upward and outward, casting deep—if implausible—shadows on the muscular fighters. One fighter is cast in shadow from above, the other from below.

Bortsi (Fighters) (ABOVE, TOP LEFT)
U.S.S.R. export to Mongolia, 1950s

Leonidas (ABOVE)
Brazil, 1930s

Splash (RIGHT)
Indonesia, 1997

Homerun *(RIGHT)*
Liggett & Myers Tobacco Co.,
U.S.A., 1950; introduced in
1886

Plus Four *(FAR RIGHT)*
Manhattan Cigar & Tobacco
Co., U.S.A., 1937

Tennismeister *(BELOW)*
Germany, 1920s

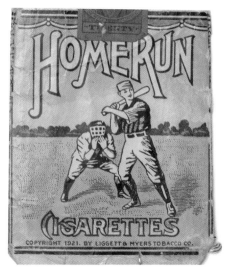

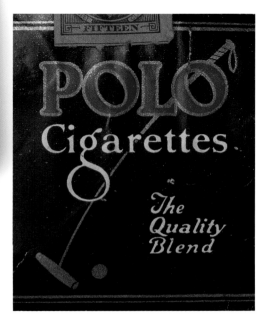

(CLOCKWISE FROM LEFT)

Polo
Liggett & Myers Tobacco Co., U.S.A., c. 1910; introduced in 1887

Top Score
Brown & Williamson Tobacco Corp., U.S.A., 1955

Sportsman
Tanzania Cigarette Co., Tanzania, 1996

Twenty Grand
Axton-Fisher Tobacco Co., U.S.A., 1932

Derby (OPPOSITE)
Successors to Douglas Rhodes & Co., India, 1950s

10 Derby CIGARETTES

Derby
VIRGINIA CIGARETTES

飛馬®

中國上海捲烟廠出品

Straight from Eden

Beasts to Blossoms

IN 1865 the Durham, North Carolina–based tobacco manufacturer John Green bought a jar of imported English mustard with a bull mascot for its brand. The bull signified strength and fortitude—good qualities for a mustard. Green decided that the bull would make an even better brand for his rolling tobacco and named his product Bull Durham. The name set Green's tobacco apart from the other Durham-based tobaccos and established a precedent for the use of animals on tobacco packaging. The bull became a symbol of muscular strength, giving a much-needed masculinity to cigarettes, which at that point were still suspected of being too effeminate for real men. When William Blackwell bought the brand in 1869, he launched a national advertising campaign that made the term a household name and turned Bull Durham into the best-selling brand of tobacco in the U.S.

Animals serve as characters and symbols that transform into visual language what can't be expressed effectively in words. Each culture has its own animal personas that have a much more prominent position in the cultural psyche than a new, unfamiliar brand ever could attain. On the 1995 package of China's Flying Horse brand, on the Chinese market since the 1960s, the horse is endowed with supersonic energy. Powered by the factories that fill the valley below, the horse stands in for China itself, leaping into the future so quickly it leaves vapor trails. On the other side of the package is an agricultural scene of lush-meadowed farms, encapsulating the yin-yang of agriculture and industry. The packaging works by tapping into a cultural iconography in ways that an export manufacturer could never have understood.

If animals tend to be used to signify characteristics of the user, plant life adds other dimensions to brand identity. A flourish of roses or lilies might indicate the addition of delicate flavoring or perfume to a turn-of-the-century brand. Flavored cigarettes were often marketed to women early in the history of cigarette packaging, when a link was made between the floral and the feminine. As packaging evolved, that association did as well. On some later packs, the women and the flowers become entwined, almost as one, and the flowers stand for something altogether different, speaking not to feminine needs but to male desire.

Darling (*ABOVE, TOP*)
Hungary, 1940s

Alligator (*ABOVE, BOTTOM*)
Larus & Brothers Co., U.S.A., 1946

Canarios (Canaries) (*LEFT*)
El Buen Tono, Mexico, 1906

Flying Horse (*OPPOSITE*)
Shanghai Cigarette Factory, China, 1995; introduced in the 1960s

85

Puppies *(ABOVE)*
Alliance Cigarette
Manufacturers,
U.S.A., 1945

Shepheard's Hotel
(RIGHT)
Dimitrino & Co.,
Germany, 1998

Man's Best Friend

The Belgian Rony of the 1940s,
its name possibly a take on
Hollywood's famous Rin Tin Tin,
features an alert-looking German
shepherd that would never let its
owner down. Canine brands also
come with other personalities:
frisky, fun-loving pet, in the U.S.
Puppies, as well as elegant status
symbol, in the high-end
Shepheard's Hotel, emblazoned
with an aristocratic Russian
wolfhound.

(CLOCKWISE FROM BELOW)

Rony
R. Geens, Belgium, 1940s

Droog *(Friend)*
*M. S. Uritzkogo, U.S.S.R.,
1980s*

Black Cat
Carreras, U.K., 1940s

Barking Dog
*Barkmahn Co., U.S.A., 1920s;
introduced in 1916*

Tiger (TOP)
BAT, U.S.A. export, 1900s;
introduced in 1895

Tegar (Tiger) (ABOVE, LEFT)
Sampoerna, Indonesia, 1996

Tiger (ABOVE, RIGHT)
P. Lorillard Tobacco Co., U.S.A., 1915

Tigres (Tigers) (OPPOSITE)
Mexico, 1995

Red Lion (LEFT, TOP)
Neyns & Lenders, U.K., 1950s

Lion (LEFT, BOTTOM)
Melikian Crg. Co., U.S.A., 1919

CIGARROS

TIGRES ᴹᴿ

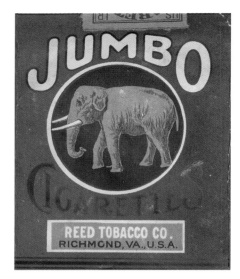

Elephants

Most animals have been anthro-pomorphized in one way or anoth-er. The elephant, in particular, is endowed with a whole range of powers and attributes that vary from culture to culture. Reed Tobacco's Jumbo brand plays on the beast's size to tout the ciga-rette's jumbo proportions, though the elephant striding across the target also suggests a hint of the upscale, sporting white hunter. A new version of Jumbo, put out by Moonlight Tobacco in 1995, fea-tures an aggressive-looking bull elephant preparing to charge right off the pack.

The elephant's hallowed place in Asian mythology earns it a more symbolic position on the Chinese pack Yin Xiang (Silver Elephant). Here the beast stands with one foot off the ground, in a gesture traditionally signifying good luck. The Indian 501 pack of cheaply made bidis, *on sale today, features Ganesh the ele-phant god.*

Red Dragon *(ABOVE, TOP LEFT)*
China, 1930s

Buffalo *(ABOVE, TOP CENTER)*
Tabacalera Hondureña,
Honduras, 1940s

Jumbo *(ABOVE, TOP RIGHT)*
Reed Tobacco Co., U.S.A., 1945

Jin Si Hou *(Golden Monkey)*
(ABOVE, LEFT)
China, 1995

Yin Xiang *(Silver Elephant)*
(ABOVE, RIGHT)
China, 1995

501 *(ABOVE)*
India, 1996

Jumbos *(OPPOSITE)*
Moonlight Tobacco Co., U.S.A., 1995

(CLOCKWISE FROM LEFT)

Camel
R. J. Reynolds, U.S.A.,
1920s; introduced in 1913

La Llama
Tabacalera del Sur, Peru,
1997

Emu
Republic Tobacco Co.,
Costa Rica, mid-1980s

Tigre (Tiger)
Tabacalera Hondureña,
Honduras, 1930s

Canada
Axton-Fisher Tobacco Co.,
U.S.A., 1930s

Monroe
1930s

Camel and Its Imitators

The popularity of Camels gave rise to dozens of imitations, such as the Costa Rican Emu, Honduran Tigre, Peruvian La Llama, and American Axton-Fisher's Canada, which pokes fun at the poker face of a Canadian Mountie. All were designed to mimic the Camel package formula: an animal or figure is placed at the center of a sparse, if slightly disproportionate landscape, possibly with some background landmarks; a stylized frame completes the effect. Camel was so successful that its own manufacturer capitalized on the formula, introducing variations on the theme to capture an ever-larger share of the market. RJR Reynold's 1996 Red Kamel, a collector's pack designed for the burgeoning Gen-X market, is a retro take on the first Camel of them all: the 1908 Red Kamel originally produced by the Turco-Russian Cigarette Company.

Red Kamel (RIGHT)
R. J. Reynolds Tobacco
Co., U.S.A., 1914;
introduced in 1908

Kamel Red (ABOVE)
R. J. Reynolds Tobacco Co., U.S.A.,
1996

Camel (ABOVE)
R. J. Reynolds Tobacco Co., U.S.A.,
2000; collector's pack designed by
Damien Hirst

Camel (ABOVE)
R. J. Reynolds Tobacco Co., U.S.A.,
2000; collector's pack designed by Nan
Goldin

Eagle Bird (ABOVE)
BAT, U.S.A. export, 1910s;
introduced in 1898

Double Eagle (RIGHT)
BAT, U.S.A. export, 1900s

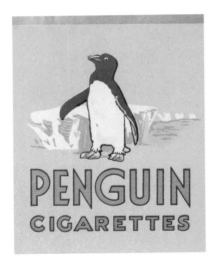

Penguin (ABOVE)
Brown & Williamson Tobacco
Corp., U.S.A., 1929

Teal (ABOVE)
Ogden of Liverpool, U.K., 1930s

Red Bird (ABOVE)
Dominion Tobacco Co., India, 1950s

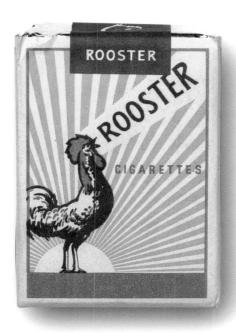

Rooster (*ABOVE*)
BAT, Kenya, 1997

Cock (*ABOVE*)
Kuo Chiang Co., China, 1930s

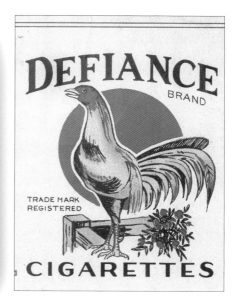

Defiance (*ABOVE*)
U.S.A., 1937

Menthorets (*LEFT*)
Rosedor Cigarette Co., U.S.A., 1928

Turkey (*ABOVE*)
Axton-Fisher Tobacco Co., U.S.A., 1936

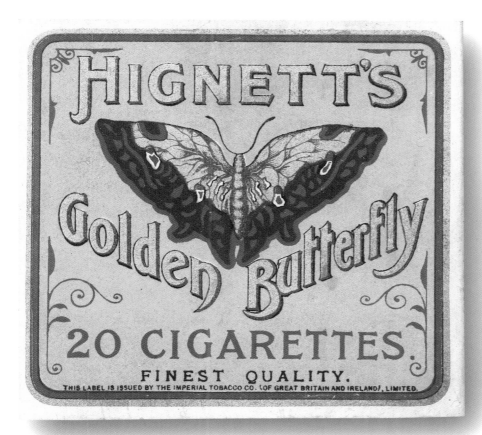

Golden Butterfly *(LEFT)*
Hignett, U.K., 1930s

Golden Bat *(BELOW)*
*Japan Tobacco, Japan, 1998;
introduced in 1906*

Honey-Toasted Tobacco
(FAR LEFT)
*Moonlight Tobacco Co., U.S.A.,
1995*

Ecstacy *(LEFT)*
*Global World Media Corp.,
U.S.A., 1997*

Mariposas *(Butterflies) (OPPOSITE)*
La Tabacalera Mexicana, Mexico, 1940

(CLOCKWISE FROM ABOVE)

Primrose
Redford & Co., U.K., 1930s

Wild Rose
Star Tobacco Co., India, 1900s

Fruits & Flowers
E. T. Pilkinton, U.S.A., 1890s

Margaritas
El Buen Tono, Mexico, 1906

Whu Dei *(Invincible Brand)*
China, 1930s

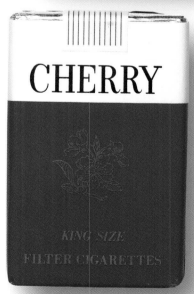

Mang Guo (Mango) *(ABOVE, LEFT)*
China, 1995

Ginseng *(ABOVE)*
China, 1998

Cherry *(FAR LEFT)*
Japan Tobacco, Japan, 1998

Beech-Nut *(LEFT)*
P. Lorillard Tobacco Co., U.S.A.,
1921

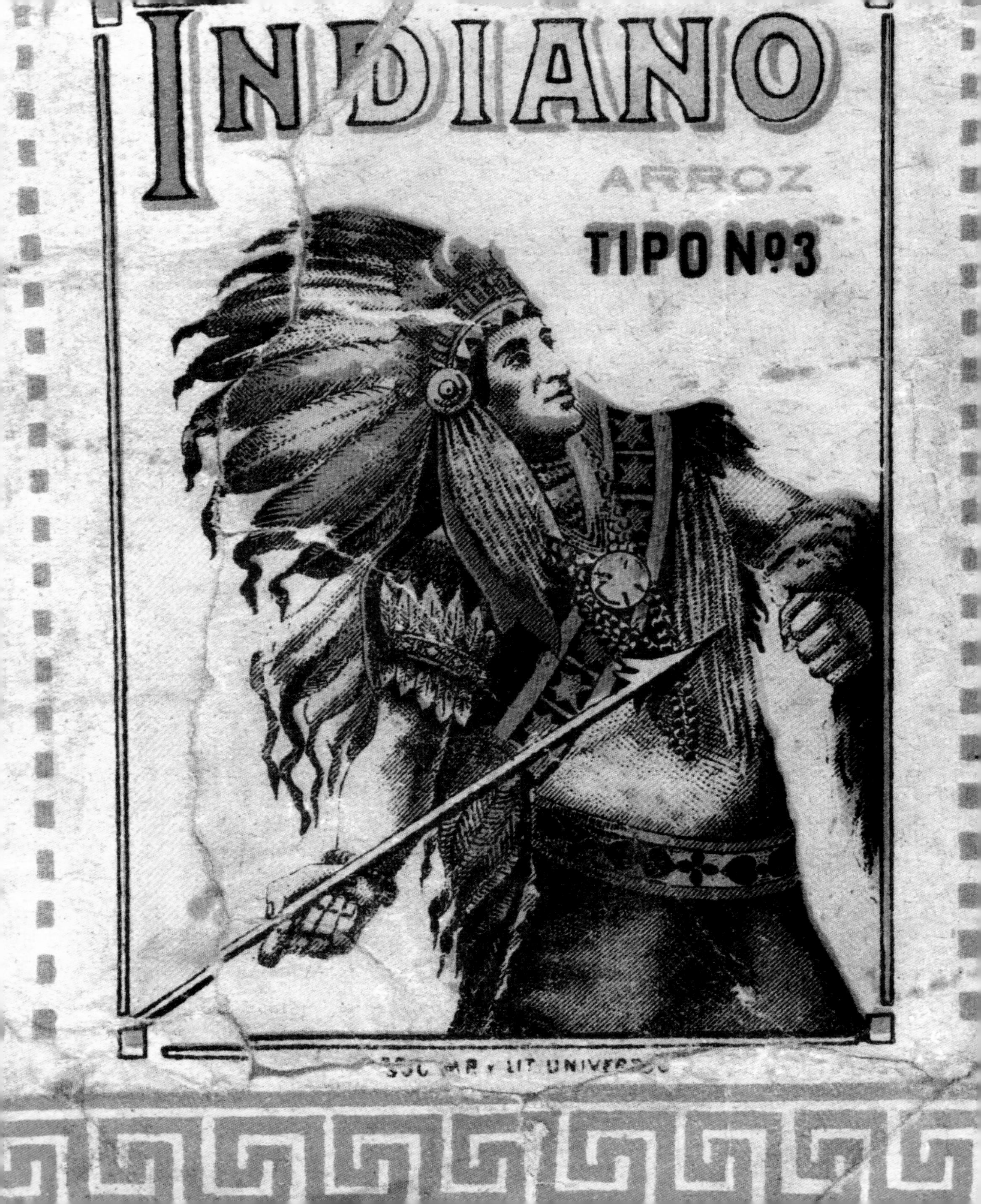
INDIANO
ARROZ
TIPO Nº3

Cigarette Indians
Packaging the American Spirit

WHEN THE U.S. INDIAN WARS ended in the 1890s, the widespread appropriation of Indians on packaging began, particularly in the States. Once they were no longer a threat, Indians were turned into icons of savage dignity and primitive purity, representing the much-romanticized era of the American frontier. They've also been used to embody other desirable qualities long purveyed in cigarette package design: freedom, masculinity, and fresh air.

The presence of the perturbed-looking chief on the One-Eleven brand from American Tobacco (launched in 1903) is mystifying unless viewed in a historical context. The chief is Powhatan, a figure crucial to the origins of tobacco farming. The father of Pocahontas, he is credited with having lent his expertise on tobacco cultivation to his son-in-law John Rolfe, the original Virginia tobacco farmer. Other examples of history-based designs are the Mexican Aztecas, a long-time brand manufactured by La Libertad and still on the market today, and the Peruvian Incas, manufactured by Empresa Nacional del Tabaco. Other tribal connections come closer to fantasy than to history. Western Tobacco's 1940s West American brand features a view of Indian life straight out of the pages of a comic book: a red-skinned warrior with eagle-feather headdress, a giant arrowhead, and Indian symbols covering a leather-brown ground.

The brand American Spirit, created by a small company as an alternative to Big Tobacco brands and popular with American college and youth markets, claims that its additive-free tobacco gives a healthier, more flavorful smoke: the Indian icon has been transformed from an emblem of ferocity to one of natural purity. The Tuscarora Indian Nation has reappropriated the Native American image for its own reservation-made brand, Pure. The package features a much lighter-skinned warrior in a slightly psychedelic-looking headdress. His demeanor suggests a new sense of sinewy strength, even personality, that is missing in the other depictions. He's the only cigarette-package Indian who looks genuinely proud and authentic, though also a little weary and just a bit cynical.

Coupon (*ABOVE*)
Liggett & Myers Tobacco Co.,
U.S.A., 1911

One-Eleven (*BELOW*)
American Tobacco Co., U.S.A.,
1922; introduced in 1903

Indiano (Indian) (*OPPOSITE*)
Avilés Hermanos y Cia., Chile,
1900s

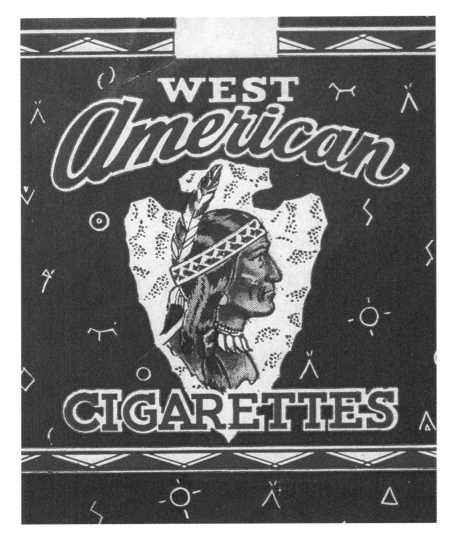

Pure *(BELOW)*
Alternative Cigarettes, U.S.A.,
1995

West American *(ABOVE)*
Western Tobacco Co., U.S.A., 1940s

American Spirit *(RIGHT)*
Santa Fe Natural Tobacco Co., U.S.A.,
2000; introduced in 1996

Pielroja *(Redskin)* *(ABOVE)*
Compañia Colombiana de
Tabaco, Colombia, 1986

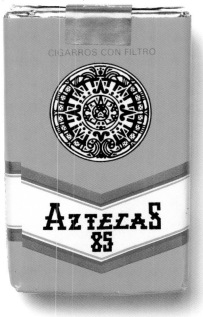

Calumet *(ABOVE)*
S. Anargyros & Co., U.S.A., 1902

Aztecas *(FAR LEFT)*
La Libertad, Mexico, 1998

Inca *(LEFT)*
*Empresa Nacional del Tabaco,
Peru, 1999*

Character Packs

Selling with Personality

GIVING INANIMATE OBJECTS PERSONALITY is nothing new in marketing, but giving personality to inanimate objects that have a life of approximately three minutes from match to stub is something else. Smokers have shown themselves more than willing to make this leap of faith. Throughout history, brands have been represented successfully by images of sailors, goddesses, girls next door, heroes, clowns, and cowboys. Smokers can match their identities to the brands they sense best represent them, or most enhance them.

The popularity of some personas shifts according to time and place, while others seem timeless. The cowboy, in various forms, played a role long before the American Marlboro Man, as evidenced by the Mexican Charros brand of 1928, which features a cowboy roping a steer, all motion and drama. The Dutch brand Caballero, still on sale today, features what could be the very same cowboy, only on a Sunday ride; now dressed in a snappy bolero suit, he sits tall in the saddle on a prancing show horse. Certain brands have isolated one element of the successful cowboy/Marlboro association, as with China's denim-printed Cowboy of the 1970s and 1980s, and Austria's denim-printed Johnny, a recently redesigned brand that was originally introduced in 1948.

Another persona that transcends eras is the clown—at times a prankster, at times endearingly innocent. Clown, an American ten-center, features a feminine mischief maker, a rose and a feather in her cap, puckering her red lips into a knowing invitation. A male variant appears in the El Salvador brand Payasos (clowns), perched on a giant balloon like an overgrown toddler. Payasos remains a popular brand, still on the market after decades of circulation.

Other personas, however, lose their appeal over time. The Dandy character popular at the turn of the century (an allusion to Oscar Wilde, who reportedly made a point of smoking cigarettes in public) was outmoded by the early 1920s. At that point the Belgian Mickey, with its jaunty, Jazz Age feel, more aptly described the era's man-about-town persona. But, strangely, there's not all that much difference between the pearl-wearing Virginia of 1948 and the blond Belinda still on sale, though Virginia was American and Belinda, Dutch. Mary Long, a Swiss brand made with Maryland tobacco that originated in the 1950s (her name is a phonetic variation on Maryland), features a slightly more confident-looking character, this time in a pearl bracelet. Her attire and coif are updated every ten years to keep her looking au courant. As she smokes, she gazes directly at the bearer of the pack, and she personifies a free and easy kind of grace. What seems most notable about all three characters is that none of them is doing anything. Female characters on cigarettes often do little more than look alluring, as intangible and unproductive as smoke.

Call for Philip Morris
Philip Morris & Co., U.S.A., 1950s

The cheery-looking character on the Philip Morris package was a real bellboy named Johnny Roventini. He was discovered in 1933, while working in his usual capacity at the New Yorker Hotel. PM's adman had been looking for an angle when he spotted Roventini—barely four feet tall in his uniform. He gave Roventini fifty cents to announce a message for Philip Morris, and the bellboy's high, vibrant voice filled the lobby. Roventini was hired instantly and paged Philip Morris on up to four live radio shows a day. Plastered on cigarette packs, billboards, and advertisements, he was the world's first living trademark.

Payasos *(Clowns)* (OPPOSITE)
El Salvador, 1995

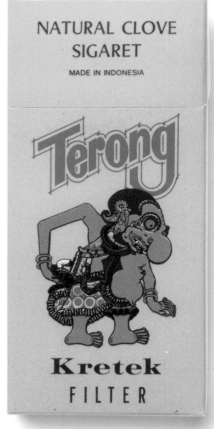

NATURAL CLOVE
SIGARET

MADE IN INDONESIA

Terong

Kretek
FILTER

Clown (ABOVE, LEFT)
*Axton-Fisher Tobacco Co., U.S.A.,
1920s*

Terong (Eggplant) (ABOVE, RIGHT)
P. T. Bentoel, Indonesia, 1998

Dandy (LEFT)
*Oriental Tobacco Co., Canada,
1903*

Guru (OPPOSITE)
India, 1998

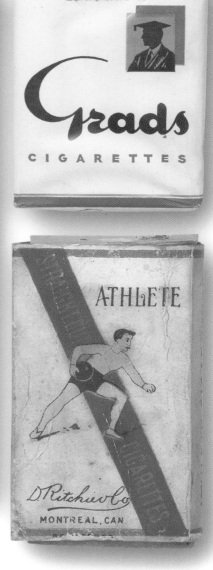

(CLOCKWISE FROM ABOVE)

Campeones (Champions)
El Buen Tono, Mexico, 1930s

Grads
Madison Tobacco Co., U.S.A., 1939

Athlete
D. Ritchieu Co., Canada, 1890s

Paymaster (OPPOSITE, LEFT)
U.K. Tobacco Co., U.K., 1930s

Orang (Pilot) (OPPOSITE, CENTER)
Indonesia, 1995

Life Guard (OPPOSITE, RIGHT)
Brown & Williamson Tobacco
Corp., U.S.A., 1935

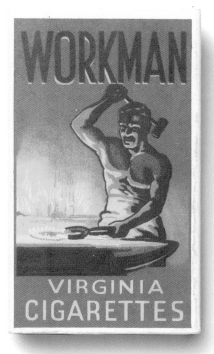

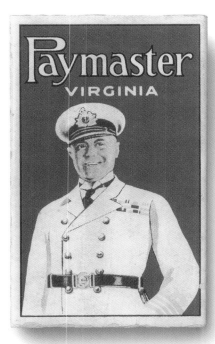

Legonaire (LEFT)
Legonaire Tobacco Corp., U.S.A., 1940

Workman (ABOVE)
Malta, 1930s

(CLOCKWISE FROM LEFT)

Johnny
*Austria Tabak, Austria, 1996;
introduced in 1948*

Cowboy
*Yichang Cigarette Factory, China,
1980s*

Caballero
*E. D. Laurens Continental,
Holland, 1998*

Charros
El Buen Tono, Mexico, 1928

Rodeio
Brazil, 1930s

El Torero *(Bullfighter)* *(OPPOSITE)*
*Compañia Durangueña, Mexico,
1911*

Raleigh

Brown & Williamson Tobacco Corp.,
U.S.A., 1944; introduced in 1928

Raleigh cigarettes featured the
royal and somewhat sober-looking
countenance of nobleman-poet-
statesman Sir Walter Raleigh, who
reputedly introduced tobacco that
he had grown in Virginia to the
court of Queen Elizabeth I. Each
time the package was updated, so
was the appearance of its figure-
head. In the 1944 design shown
here, his coat of arms and car-
touche have been roughed up
around the edges, his hat has
received a jaunty feather, and his
torso appears broader than in ear-
lier versions, in keeping with the
broad-shouldered fashions of the
mid-1940s.

Johnnie Walker (FAR LEFT)
Falk Tobacco Co., U.S.A., 1927;
introduced in 1911

Paul Jones (LEFT)
Continental Tobacco Co., U.S.A., 1927

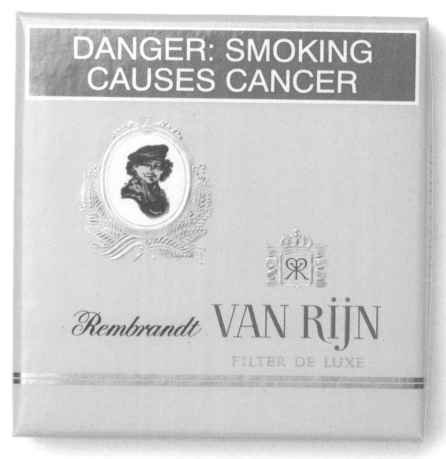

John Peel *(ABOVE)*
*John Peel, successors to Douglas Rhodes
& Co., India, 1950s*

Rembrandt Van Rijn *(RIGHT)*
Rothmans, South Africa, 1997

Waverley *(BELOW, LEFT)*
Lambert & Butler, U.K., 1940

Omar Sharif *(BELOW, RIGHT)*
KT & G, Korea, 1999; introduced in 1995

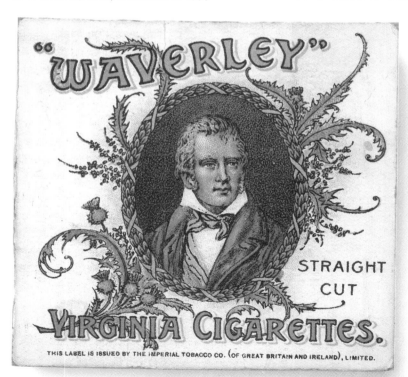

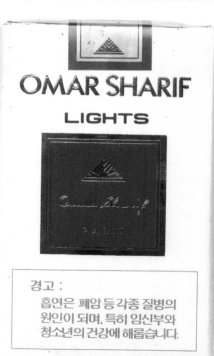

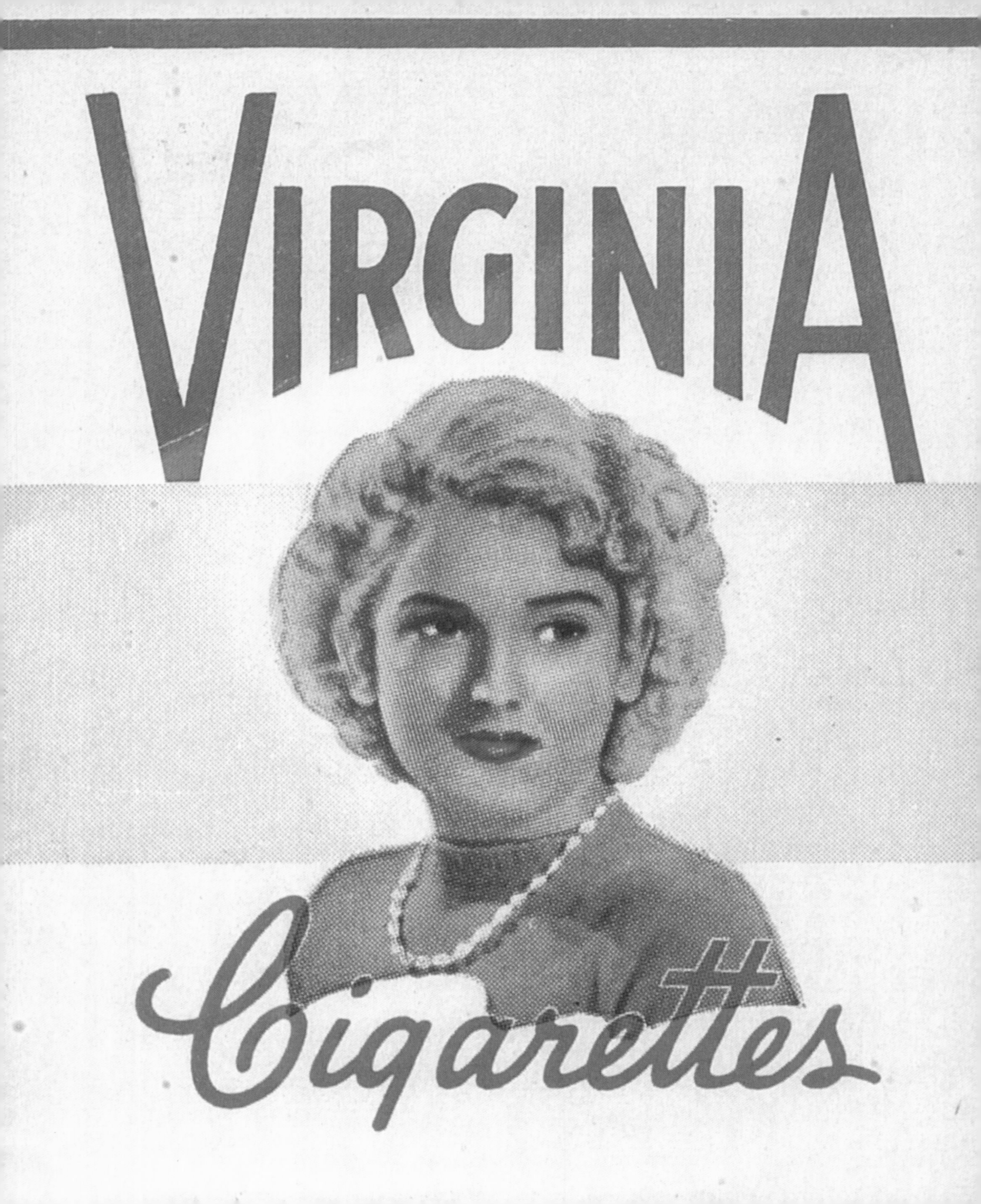
VIRGINIA
Cigarettes

Yolanda *(ABOVE, LEFT)*
Brazil, 1930s

Olga *(ABOVE, RIGHT)*
Brazil, 1930s

Mary Long *(RIGHT)*
BAT, Switzerland, 1997;
introduced in the 1950s

Virginia *(OPPOSITE)*
Tobacco Blending Corp., U.S.A.,
1948

George Sand *(ABOVE)*
Poland, 1999

Belinda *(RIGHT)*
BAT, Holland, 1999

Wish You Were Here

Location, Location, Location

A *SENSE OF PLACE* evokes universal emotions: pride, nostalgia, homesickness, longing. How geography is used on cigarette packaging hasn't changed all that much over the years. In some packages it's used to commemorate a vanished civilization, as in Allen & Ginter's Dixie brand, released after the Civil War. The entire design has a wistfulness to it: the small trademark cameo at the bottom-left corner, the engraving-style scroll and thin line work. Dixie wasn't so much a place as a way of life: as encapsulated in this brand, it's gone but not forgotten.

Serving a different purpose is El Buen Tono's 1904 Covadonga, a souvenir package from Mexico. The cover features a beautifully rendered church built at the entrance to a cavern: these specific details attest to the fact that the place depicted is a real place. It was in this cavern that townspeople witnessed the divine appearance of the Virgin Mary. What better way to contemplate such a miracle than with a cigarette?

Nostalgia sells across many borders, though to be an effective tool each locale must capture a regionally appropriate feel. Liggett & Myers's Old Mill of 1894 pays homage to the fast-disappearing sight of the quaint old mill by the stream, surrounded by lots of greenery and no people. The Latin American equivalent also hearkens back to simpler, rural times, but with a thatched-roof cabin nestled by a stand of palm trees, somewhere in the peaceful countryside. The Cuban José L. Piedra brand of the 1940s and the Panamanian Bohio brand of the 1950s feature two variations of this singular scene, both cast in the warm, shadowy light of a late afternoon's setting sun.

One brand to proudly insist on its own appeal despite a well-known twist of fate is China's commemorative Chairman Mao Memorial Hall package, a souvenir of the landmark in which Mao-tse Tung is buried. The package features a picture of the hall in regal gold, set on a background of pure, heavenly white. Mao loved cigarettes and was famous for chain smoking until he contracted lung cancer. Given the circumstances, the brand becomes an ironically fitting celebration of a public figure.

Bohio (ABOVE)
Tabacalera Istmeña, Panama, 1950s

Old Mill (BELOW)
Liggett & Myers Tobacco Co., U.S.A., 1928; introduced in 1894

José L. Piedra (OPPOSITE)
José Piedra, Cuba, 1940s

Mexico (*ABOVE*)
Ta Hwa Tobacco Co., China, 1930s

Continental (*OPPOSITE*)
Souza Cruz, Brazil, 1930s

CIGARRILLOS

Istmeños

TIPO AMERICANO
EXTRA FINOS

Istmeños (*ABOVE*)
Tabacalera Istmeña, Panama, 1940s

La Cubana (*RIGHT*)
Uruguay, 1995

SOUZA CRUZ
Cigarros
Continental
Cia de Cigarros Souza Cruz

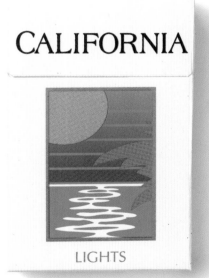

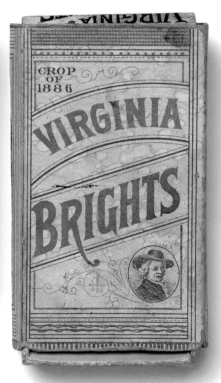

Virginia Brights
Allen & Ginter Tobacco Co., U.S.A.,
1889; introduced in 1879

California
Philip Morris & Co., U.S.A., 1992

Florida
Brazil, 1920s

Florida
Egypt, 1979

Texas
Brazil, 1930s

The American Way

The American way of life is pitched by brands all over the world. Brooklyn, a French brand of the 1990s, and Hollywood, a Brazilian brand from the 1940s (still on sale today), feature little more than the brand names themselves but are certain to cue a whole range of hopes and daydreams. Philip Morris's California brand of 1992 adds a sun reflecting on the water to support the clear and simple statement of the brand name. By contrast, Lorillard's Newport may have been named for the wealthy Rhode Island enclave, but that association has been progressively pushed into the background. The original pack, introduced in 1956, reflects the original pitch: the elegant, by-the-sea life of leisure is conjured up by the abstracted, wind-filled sail and the easy marine blue of the package.

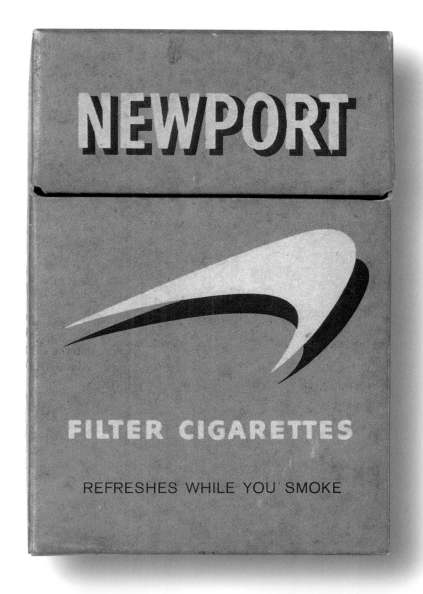

Newport *(ABOVE, RIGHT)*
P. Lorillard Tobacco Co., U.S.A., 1956

Hollywood *(RIGHT)*
Souza Cruz, Brazil, 1940s

Brooklyn *(FAR RIGHT)*
SEITA, France, 1998

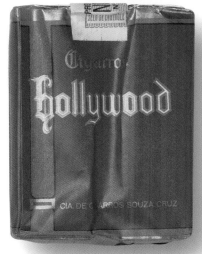

TABACO
POLA DE SIERO
EL BUEN TONO, S. A.
PROVEEDORES DE LA REAL CASA DE ESPAÑA.
COVADONGA
PAPEL CANARIOS
MARCA IND. REC. Nº 6664.-7 SEP. 1906.

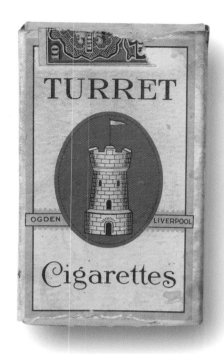

Turret (*ABOVE*)
Ogden of Liverpool, U.K. export to
Canada, 1910s

Victory (*ABOVE*)
BAT, Cambodia, 1998

The Chairman Mao Memorial Hall
(*ABOVE*)
China, 1999

Hang Ta Shan (*Red Pagoda Mountain*)
China, 1996

China's enormous population of smokers can choose
from thousands of different brands of cigarettes. The
proliferation of brands traces back to Mao, an inveter-
ate smoker, who wanted his people to have one arena
in which they could exercise personal preference. It is
a Chinese custom to give cigarette packages as gifts
and as souvenirs of faraway places. The in-laws, for
instance, might come to visit bearing cigarette brands
from their own city. There are brands to celebrate
events and ideological triumphs as well as brands to
commemorate landmarks, mountains, temples, bodies
of water, cities, and even tiny country villages. Many
interweave traditional colors and numerology into
their designs: eight is a traditionally lucky number.
On the Hang Ta Shan brand, the red pagoda soars
eight stories into the sky, taller than the mountains in
the distance as it rises through the smokelike clouds.

Covadonga (*OPPOSITE*)
El Buen Tono, Mexico, 1904

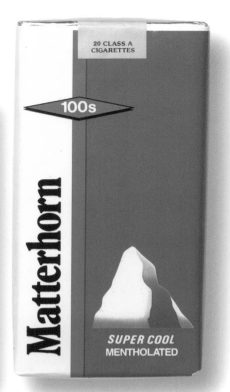

(CLOCKWISE FROM ABOVE)

Suez
Egypt, 1970s

Alpine
*Philip Morris & Co., U.S.A., 1995;
introduced in 1958*

Matterhorn
Malaysia, 1997

Krakatoa
P. T. Bentoel, Indonesia, 1998

Abu Nakhla
Blue Nile Cigarette Co., Sudan, 1930s

Urca
Brazil, 1930s

K-2 *(OPPOSITE)*
Pakistan, 1980; introduced in 1950s

124 *Wish You Were Here*

Capitol *(OPPOSITE)*
Malta, 1930s

Metropol *(RIGHT)*
China, 1920s

The Waldorf-Astoria *(BELOW, CENTER)*
U.S.A., 1955

Skyline *(BELOW, RIGHT)*
Tobacco Blending Corp., U.S.A., 1935

City *(BELOW)*
Moonlight Tobacco Co., U.S.A., 1995

The monolithic skyscraper on the retro City pack has a brooding quality straight out of film noir. Introduced in 1995, the design pays homage to the machine age as conceived by Norman Bel Geddes, who designed similarly stripped-down skyscrapers for his City of Tomorrow at the 1939 New York world's fair. The height and shape of the building play with the length of the cigarettes, which as 100s are taller than the norm.

Pink

Superlatives

"THAT PACK HAS TO STAND FOR SOMETHING," said a Philip Morris executive in 1971. To make that easier, some cigarette packages simply spell it out. As cigarette packaging developed, the challenge was to make a package's appeal clear in one or two words. Culture by culture, brand names began to tap into universals, vernaculars, and slang. The more evocative brand names might describe human qualities or even higher aspirations. Others describe some quality of the cigarette itself. For example, Miniature brand, released by Britain's F. & J. Smith at the turn of the century, was sold at theaters; their tiny size made them ideal for a smoking break during intermission.

The art of trademarking, combining shrewd market sense with a little bit of alchemy, is both subtle and highly developed within cigarette packaging. The best brand names offer something far more than a cigarette, encapsulating an entire universe of potential associations. Instant recognition by consumers was always a goal: to make a brand name so instantly recognizable that it became a stand-in for the word *cigarette* itself, as Frigidaire became the synonym for *refrigerator* in 1950s America.

Cigarette brands seek to inspire the buyer's sense of loyalty by praising the smoker's own superior taste along with the taste of the cigarette itself. The Argentine brand Originales from the mid-1930s implied that whoever smoked them would also be an individual of original distinction. The Cuban brand Populares (The People's Brand) entered the Cuban market after the revolution and remains on sale today. Its name asserted its claim to the market without question, and it remains one of the country's most popular local brands.

Other brand names seek to add layers to the experience of smoking. Sublimes, introduced by the Mexican company El Buen Tono at the turn of the century, gives that lofty term a sensual spin when coupled with the teasing pose of the package's mantilla-wearing maiden. The same company's Sabrosos (Savories) brand of the same era describes the flavor of the tobacco but also evokes far more. The package features a young man, dapperly dressed but still somewhat innocent in his short pants. He's depicted trying what is perhaps his first smoke. The image gives the name a sense of nostalgia, evoking the piquancy of a boy's tentative initial explorations of the rituals of manhood.

How completely different is the Japanese brand Pink, with the exuberant simplicity of its saturated pink package. An American expression of the time might have inspired it; "in the pink" means feeling successful, prosperous, and healthy—qualities highly valued in postwar Japanese culture. A sense of triumph and rosy-cheeked health is contained within the small confines of a cigarette pack.

Sub-Rosa *(ABOVE)*
P. Lorillard Tobacco Co., U.S.A., 1909; introduced in 1885

Originales *(BELOW)*
Argentina, 1935

Pink *(OPPOSITE)*
Ryukyu Tobacco Co., Okinawa, 1950s

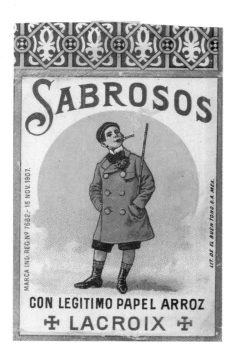

Caprichos *(OPPOSITE)*
El Buen Tono, Mexico, 1940s

Sabrosos *(Savories)* *(ABOVE)*
El Buen Tono, Mexico, 1907

Sweet Caporal *(ABOVE)*
Kinney Brothers Tobacco Works,
U.S.A., 1890s; introduced in 1860s,
best-selling brand of the 1870s

Sublimes *(ABOVE, RIGHT)*
El Buen Tono, Mexico, 1905

Sincere *(RIGHT)*
Brown & Williamson Tobacco Corp.,
U.S.A., 1950

Imparciales *(FAR LEFT)*
Argentina, 1995

Particulares *(LEFT)*
Argentina, 1995

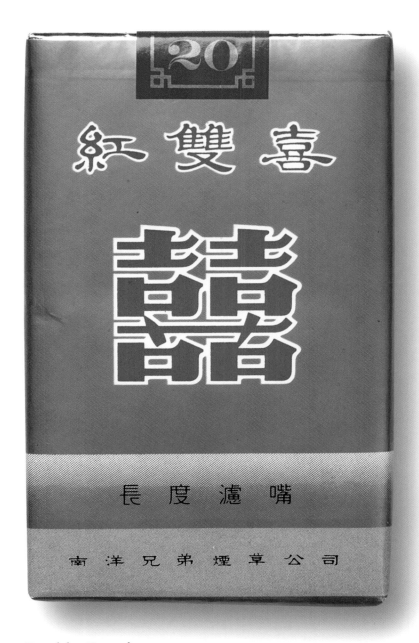

Freedom (*ABOVE*)
Rothmans, Australia, 1998

Peace (*BELOW*)
*Japanese Tobacco Monopoly, Japan, 1945;
introduced in 1920 to commemorate the end
of World War I*

Double Happiness
China, 1998

*Double Happiness was introduced by the Chinese company Nanyang
Brothers Tobacco, which had weathered the early- and mid-
twentieth-century battles against BAT. The brand is based on a
Chinese custom: Chinese often write the character for happiness
twice, in the hope that more happiness will come their way.
Double Happiness fuses the characters with the traditional Chinese
colors for good fortune, crimson and gold. The 1990s brand, with
its bold graphics and characters that practically jump off the paper,
is extremely popular today.*

Kool

*Brown & Williamson Tobacco Corp.,
U.S.A., 1944; introduced in 1933*

To bolster their new menthol brand's
position in the mid-1940s market,
Brown & Williamson took the penguin right off their brand of Penguin
cigarettes and placed him on the
back of their new Kool brand. Not
only did the penguin mascot
effectively convey the cooling nature
of the minty fresh Kools, he also
became a popular advertising
character. In the era of Mickey and
Minnie Mouse, he got a mate as
well as a name: though only Willie
the penguin appeared on the package, advertisements featured Millie
the penguin as well. The brand soon
dominated the menthol market.

First (*BELOW, LEFT*)
Ryukyu Tobacco Co., Okinawa, 1950s

Sensation (*BELOW, CENTER*)
*P. Lorillard Tobacco Co., U.S.A., 1942;
introduced in 1938*

Populares (*The People's Brand*)
(*BELOW, RIGHT*)
Cuba, 1998; introduced in 1960s

Novi (*New*) (*ABOVE*)
U.S.S.R., 1950s

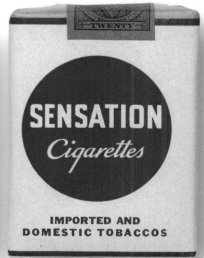

KING SIZE

The Anti-Packs
Selling with Secrets and Slang

AS AN ALTERNATIVE TO THE USUAL PACKAGING, with its earnest typography and common-denominator themes, some firms flaunt brands with attitude. Batt Brothers' Wooden-Kimona Nails of 1923 plays off a slang expression of the day, while G. A. Georgopulos's Brand X of 1960 takes a wise-guy stance, poking fun at the Madison Avenue advertising campaigns that oozed snob appeal and pretentiously touted fake marketing science. Both use text to further the gimmick, and both make use of colloquial expressions. In gutter-speak, a "wooden kimona" was a coffin. The back of the package features an epitaph as recited by the smoking skeleton on the cover, who casually leans against the cigarette-patterned frame:

> Stop here a moment and cast an eye
> As you were once so once was I
> As I am now so you will be
> Smoke up before you follow me.

Though responding to the wave of health warnings emerging in the 1920s and 1930s, the verse expresses a fatalistic stance more than an anti-smoking one. Brand X, poking fun at the new vernacular of postwar advertising, sidesteps any issue of health, adopting a tone of high irony instead. The brand's self-mocking slogan is "For the Man Who Is Satisfied With Nothing Less Than Second Best." Despite their appearance, Cancer cigarettes of 1966 were packaged in all sincerity; the design was meant to make a smoker pause long enough to break the habit. The design is often held up as the height of cynicism, yet the more the debate over how to regulate cigarettes rages on, the more relevant it seems.

The tradition of focusing heavily on nonverbal symbols in export markets has found some sophisticated interpretations. To give smokers the sense of being privy to secret information, symbols or numbers stand in for brand names. The 234 brand, currently on sale in Indonesia, implies that the brand contains a coveted secret formula, something so exclusive it can't be given a name—the 007 of cigarettes. The Deco-styled 43-70 from Argentina has a similar aura. India has its 222 brand; Germany, its Eckstein No. 5, which plays off the cachet of Chanel.

If, on the other hand, you want to cut the pretense entirely and get to the point, reach for Death, a brand from Holland featuring a skull and crossbones. Instead of fantasies involving secret codes, the brand delivers honesty. Compared to the loaded imagery usually favored in cigarette packaging, such a message is almost too direct to grasp.

Snooty (ABOVE)
Snooty Cigarettes, U.S.A., 1937

Magic (BELOW)
U.K., 1999

LD (OPPOSITE)
NIS, Yugoslavia, 1965

135

Wooden-Kimona Nails (ABOVE)
Batt Brothers Tobacco Co., U.S.A.,
1935; introduced in 1923

Carioca (RIGHT)
Brazil, 1920s

Go To Hell (FAR RIGHT)
GTH, U.S.A., 1987

Horse Shit *(RIGHT)*
Mexico, 1998

Along with Horse Shit came Chicken Shit, Cangaroo Shit, and others: Mexican joke wrappers from the 1970s meant to slip around existing American cigarette packs. The language on Horse Shit is a straight parody of the language on a package of Camels, with intentional misspellings and mistakes. "Not a fart in a boxload," the slogan trumpets, though the illustration contradicts the claim.

Death *(LEFT)*
Holland, 1990

Cancer *(ABOVE)*
Pacific Tobacco Co., U.S.A., 1966

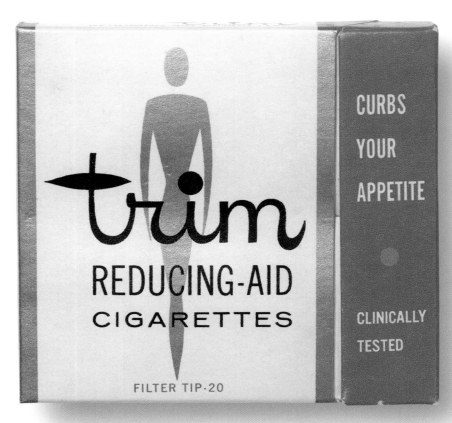

Trim
Cornell Drug Corp., U.S.A., 1960

Introduced by the Cornell Drug Corporation in 1960, Trim joined the ranks of cigarettes purporting to have medical benefits. Aimed directly at women and capitalizing on their insecurities, the package features a whisper of a female form, along with the slogans "curbs your appetite" and "clinically tested." Trim wasn't the first brand to assert that it would help women maintain their figures, but its claim was unusually audacious. Was the brand ever clinically tested? Even if it wasn't, the design and coloration of the package would fit perfectly on a drugstore counter.

Hed Kleer (ABOVE)
Hed Kleer Tobacco Corp., U.S.A., 1940s; introduced in 1936

Pure (ABOVE)
Tobacco Alternatives, U.S.A., 1995

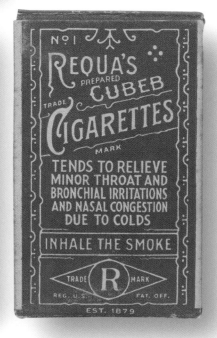

Requa's Cubeb (ABOVE)
Requa Manufacturing Co., U.S.A., 1891

Herbal Gold
Tobacco Alternatives, U.S.A., 1998

Long Life
Taiwan Tobacco & Wine Monopoly,
Taiwan, 1998

Var Chakra
India, 1950s

B&H

TOBACCO SERIOUSLY
DAMAGES HEALTH

No
Name
Cigarettes

B & H *(FAR LEFT)*
Benson & Hedges, U.K., 1998

No Name *(LEFT)*
Brown & Williamson Tobacco Corp.,
U.S.A., 1950

Brand "X" *(BELOW)*
G. A. Georgopulo & Co., U.S.A., 1960

KING SIZE/FILTER TIPPED

For the Man Who Is Satisfied With
Nothing Less Than Second Best

BRAND
"X"
CIGARETTES

Eckstein No. 5 *(ABOVE, TOP LEFT)*
Reemtsma Hamburg, Germany, 1998;
introduced in 1860s

1 *(ABOVE, TOP RIGHT)*
Greece, 1995

Dji Sam Soe (234) *(ABOVE)*
P. T. Sampoerna, Indonesia, 1995

222 *(RIGHT)*
India, 1992

43-70
Argentina, 1997

A Collector's Guide

CIGARETTE PACKAGES ARE VALUABLE LINKS to popular culture, designed to be disposable yet often enduring far longer than intended. As collectibles, they are readily available and generally pretty affordable. Packs from the last century may cost hundreds of dollars, but a terrific collection can be built solely on more common packs, which usually cost between five and twenty-five dollars. Among the factors determining price is the condition of a package: those still unopened, with the tax stamp intact, fetch higher prices. Flats (press sheets that came off the printer but never made it onto the package) are common and tend to be in better shape than packs, but they are also less valuable.

For hard-to-find vintage packages, flea markets and conventions of paper or ephemera collectors had traditionally been the best sources. But now, as with so many other fields of collecting, the Internet has begun giving collectors a global reach. Of the many auction sites online, none comes close to eBay (www.ebay.com) for the number and variety of cigarette packages posted for sale. (Type the key word *cigarette* into eBay's search engine, and it will list more items than can be found in most flea markets.) Collectors' clubs, which often publish newsletters and hold swap meets, offer another venue for exchanging information on current and vintage cigarette packages. Three of the most popular clubs are:

Cigarette Pack Collectors Association

> 61 Searle Street
> Georgetown, Massachusetts 01833
> U.S.A.
> http://members.aol.com/cigpack/index.html

Cigarette Packet Collectors of Great Britain

> Warden's Flat
> 33/43 Lincoln's Inn Fields
> London WC2A 3PN
> U.K.

ACECA-BR

> (South American Cigarette Pack Collectors Club)
> CX. Postal 236—Centro
> São Paulo, Brazil
> www.brasil.terravista.pt/praiabrava/1169/aceca.htm

Index

(Page numbers in *italic* refer to illustrations.)

A Note about the Captions

Unless otherwise indicated, the date in the caption indicates the year that the package illustrated was on sale.

Acknowledgments

MICHAEL THIBODEAU thanks everyone who added insight and items to the cigarette-package collection shown in this book. And especially his family, who has always supported his appreciation of things viewed in a different light.

JANA MARTIN thanks, in particular, Harold Martin and Nathaniel Knight for their historical perspective; and Danny Blume, Myrna Martin, and Nancy Martin, as always.

EDITOR: Nancy Grubb
DESIGNER: Patricia Fabricant
PRODUCTION EDITOR: Max Dickstein
PRODUCTION MANAGER: Louise Kurtz
DIGITAL PHOTOGRAPHY: Elliot Morgan/Blink Studio

First edition
10 9 8 7 6 5 4 3 2 1

Library of Congress Cataloging-in-Publication Data
Thibodeau, Michael.
  Smoke gets in your eyes : branding and design in cigarette packaging / Michael Thibodeau, Jana Martin.
     p. cm.
  ISBN 0-7892-0640-4
  1. Cigarettes—Packaging. I. Martin, Jana. II. Title.
TS2260.T48 2000
741.6'92—dc21   00-032289

DATE DUE

APR 1 2002	ILL 5162214 PGP
MAY 09 2005	RR#4347244 PPN
JUL 28 2006	
OCT 29 2006	
MAR 22 2011	
GAYLORD	PRINTED IN U.S.A.